Q

This is to certify that
this book is number 884
of a signed limited edition
of 1000 copies only.

Desmond with the original briefcase. ***From Russia With Love***

Q

The Biography of Desmond Llewelyn

Desmond Llewelyn

Sandy Hernu

Sandy Hernu.

S. B. Publications

First published in 1999 by S. B. Publications,
19 Grove Road, Seaford. East Sussex. BN25 1TP

It should be noted that any comments made by the author about the James Bond 007 films do not reflect the opinions of EON Productions.

ISBN 1 85770 187 9 (paperback)
ISBN 1 85770 205 0 (hardback)

Produced by Design 2 Output
60 Greenway, Old Town, Eastbourne, East Sussex BN20 8UL

Printed by Adland Print Group Ltd
Unit 11, Bellingham Trading Estate, Franthorne Way, London SE6 3BX

CONTENTS

Front Cover: Desmond and a selection of gadgets from Q Branch.
Back Cover: With Pierce Brosnan in *Tomorrow Never Dies.*
Title Page: Desmond with the original briefcase - *From Russia With Love.*

ACKNOWLEDGEMENTS

This biography of Q could never have been written without the co-operation and generosity of all the people involved with EON Productions. In particular, I would like to thank Meg Simmonds, who spent hours sorting through the Bond film archives for relevant information and Amanda Schofield, the Publicity Manager for EON. Also to those who made my visits to Pinewood Studios so enjoyable and answered my endless questions.

I would like to thank Desmond's two sons, Ivor and Justin, together with the rest of their families, for the help and kindness they have shown throughout.

A special mark of appreciation must go to my husband, Jeffrey, whose support and computer skills, (which far outweigh mine) made the whole thing possible.

And finally to my editor, Sharon Searle, who managed to pull the manuscript into shape.

JUST A QUICK WORD...

. . . from The Author

Desmond Llewelyn may or may not be a household name, but his voice is familiar and the crooked smile strikes a chord. Just who is this craggy, white haired Welshman, obversely epitomising an English gentleman and without a trace of modesty, claiming to be the most famous small-part actor in the world?

For over thirty-five years Desmond has played Q, the gadget-minded boffin without whom, James Bond 007 would have been annihilated way back in the 1960's. Like Q he is mildly eccentric. Unlike Q he finds the simplest of gadgets difficult to understand. Now at eighty-five, with his 17th Bond film tucked safely under his belt, he finds his rise to fame in the last few years, inexplicable. Why, when he's been around for so long?

Perhaps it's because he has sixty years of acting to his credit, although during that time he had no major roles, no meaty character parts and no scandals to pin to his chest. He professes to have been 'discovered' on at least half a dozen occasions, yet ongoing recognition yo-yo'd tantalisingly out of reach. But although small, the parts rolled in as his tenacious climb zig-zagged through theatre, films, television and people - and ultimately, Bond.

Q's humble origins began, for me, in 1962 with the second 007 film, From Russia with Love. *The previous actor, Peter Burton, who played Major Boothroyd (subsequently Q) in* Dr No, *was unavailable for filming and I jumped at the opportunity to take his place. At Pinewood, the director Terence Young, asked how I was going to portray Q, then simultaneously announced he wanted him to be played as a Welshman. Maybe he'd remembered how passionate I could be about my ancestry and reckoned I'd be only too happy to follow his wishes. He was wrong and a disagreement ensued. My interpretation of the character was that of a toffee-nosed Englishman. At the risk of losing the part and with silent apologies to my native land, I launched into Q's lines using the thickest and worst Welsh accent, followed by the same in precision English.*

As Desmond pauses for a minute to down another Guinness, my pen works furiously to capture these peripheral tales. He is, I note, larger in life, a comfortable companion and an amusing raconteur.

Sandy Hernu.

. . . from Roger Moore

I first met Desmond when we appeared in *Ivanhoe* in the 1950's and then we briefly came into contact again when he was in Rome filming *Cleopatra*. Disappointingly, Q did not make an appearance in my first 007 movie, *Live And Let Die*, but I got to know him well when we worked together on the next six James Bond productions. This spanned a period of about ten years and began with *The Man With The Golden Gun* in 1974. Desmond was an absolute delight to work with although he often seemed perplexed by my inability to take life too seriously and my overriding sense of humour. He, on the other hand, had the type of character that begged to be wound up and I could never resist the temptation to do so. I must say, he took it all in very good heart.

I do recall him having a 'thing' against wearing shorts on screen. So, naturally, if a chance occurred for Q to show his legs, the director and I would get together and inform Desmond that Q's scene definitely required shorts. He used to get so flustered at the prospect.

Roger Moore with the Acrostar mini jet from *Octopussy*.

Sometimes, he would have difficulty with his lines concerning the gadgets, which was not surprising as many of them were technically 'way out'. He used to sit and mumble to himself in a corner, or pace up and down the studio, trying to learn his words. This led to me writing several pages of sheer gobbledegook, getting them typed and then adding them to his script. You should have seen Desmond's face when he thought he had to learn all these extra lines!

But we had some fun and I must say, one of the things I missed most about leaving Bond, was leaving Q.

. . . and Desmond Llewelyn

I've always wanted to write a book. Not surprisingly, friends and family were rather astounded when I mentioned the idea. This was simply because I can neither spell nor punctuate and have always been a terrible letter writer. Nevertheless, since childhood I have compiled 'great works' in the form of well thumbed scrapbooks. It began with family snapshots and favourite animals, then graduated to world speed records, theatre stars and a catalogue of every Welsh rugger match 1928 - 1932, including photos. After I'd joined RADA in 1934, my literary leanings manifested themselves in pages and pages of press cuttings, theatre programmes and stage photographs - I was much too busy to write a single word.

The chance to scribe my autobiography presented itself when I became a Prisoner of War in 1940. There was just one small problem. At 26, I hadn't really done anything very exciting with my life and therefore, had nothing to write about. The ink dried on the pen, the paper remained blank and after a great deal of thought both were firmly discarded.

Some thirty years later, I made another autobiographical attempt and got as far as finishing one chapter. Elated, I handed it to the family to read and waited for their comments. None came; their silence was deafening. Eventually, I asked what they thought of the first bit. Looking rather bored, one of them returned the pile of pages and said, "Well, it does rather go on - there's an awful lot of waffle, which is OK when you speak, but...!" The chapter gravitated to the back of the cupboard and is still there, gathering dust.

I wish I had Roger Moore's ability. He made any task look so effortless and wrote that fictitious script for Q, which he mentions, in about ten minutes. His touches of light-hearted humour diffused many of the tense situations that can occur when filming, for no matter how busy he was, Roger always found time for other people. I remember when he was in the midst of filming *Moonraker*, he overheard me complaining about my agent. Within twenty-four hours he'd arranged a meeting for me with his own agent, Denis Salinger - I'll always be eternally grateful for his kindness.

But back to a book, this book, not by me, but Sandy Hernu. I first met Sandy after she'd written a script for a historical video and I did the voice-over. Over a series of lunchtime sandwiches, we discovered a pleasant camaraderie and at the launch of the video (at Herstmonceux Castle, in Sussex), she approached me about the possibility of writing my biography. Since then, Sandy has spent hours listening to my stories, memories and general mind wanderings in order to present my life - without the waffle.

The makings of an actor. Desmond aged eight, with his sister Noreen.

- 1 -

BACKCLOTH

"Above all, I'm a passionate Welshman.
This is where my roots lie."

- 1 -
BACKCLOTH

It's about two miles from Newport to Malpas. Today, the green fields that divided them have vanished. Even the bees have become urban little creatures and no longer hum gently on the lacy caps of wild elder, but instead buzz fussily over the choicest rose. Roads have replaced footpaths once trodden by children as they gathered blackberries, wearing stained and puckered pinafores. The warm smell and inquisitive gaze of cattle is no more. But the view beyond those distant hills, mountains and Newport itself, is immeasurably better. A hundred years ago tall blackened chimneys, faceless sentinels, stood outlined against the sky - stark and unforgiving. Their smoke, a dense looking matter, would bring a dryness to the throat, a smell to the nostrils, a greyness to the washing line. The muffled noise of constantly worked machinery carried on the wind from the hills, across streams to beyond, left no man or woman in doubt. This was where industrial Wales began. This was where each valley held rich seams of coal and where men, like captured rabbits, burrowed through the depths of the earth to extract it. This was where the winding passage of a river, a road or a railway carried the trucks of black gold elsewhere and made others prosper.

Those very children that gathered blackberries probably had brothers, not more than ten years old, working in the mines alongside fathers, uncles and cousins. Today the air is fresher, cleaner now the industry - like the green fields at Malpas - has gone. What remains are the memories.

The Aberdare Valley lies about twenty miles west of Malpas. By the middle of the 19th century, the once sleepy hamlets reverberated with noise and activity as more than twenty collieries were established to mine the area's prolific quantities of coal. The local inhabitants provided cheap labour. It's here at Aberdare, splintered amongst the shadowy hills and coombs, amongst the Welsh people, the coal dust and the spirits of yesteryear, that Desmond Llewelyn's significant past surfaces with his great grandfather.

In 1806, Edward Llewelyn was born into Aberdare's rapidly expanding mining community. His childhood and brief schooling, such as it may have been, ended at the age of ten when the youngster was sent to work in the pits, his earnings contributing to the meagre family wage. He could neither read nor write. At twenty, whilst continuing as a collier, he took on the tenancy of The Duffryn Arms, a small pub situated in a hamlet a few miles from Aberdare. That same year he married Jane Williams who, like Edward, was illiterate, but hard working and eager to help her husband in the running of The Duffryn Arms, where the newly-weds made their home. As the archives only list Edward as being a publican/collier, we must presume he continued with his dual employment throughout his life perhaps because it brought in some extra cash. This must have been sorely needed for he and Jane had four daughters, Elizabeth, Mary, Lydia and Margaret and three sons, John, Llewelyn and baby William. Other than a birth date there is no further mention of William and therefore, it is possible he died in infancy. The livelihood of his elder brothers, John and Llewelyn, would undoubtedly follow that of their father.

From the mid 19th century records, it's evident that mining had become an increasingly hazardous occupation and colliers were being exposed to indescribable working conditions. Generally the fault lay with zealous pit owners, anxious to maximise their profits and meet the rising demand for coal, neglecting many of the safety aspects; disasters, even deaths, became commonplace.

In 1845, an accident at the Duffryn Colliery in Aberdare caused twenty-eight people to lose their lives, among them were two nine-year old boys. After many months, the gathering waves of concern were about to break and a specialist jury was summoned to examine the situation. This included prominent members of the coal industry and a mineral agent, John Nixon. A report on their meeting suggests:-

> 'The jury criticized the ventilation which allowed gas to seep into the tram roads from old workings. However, they did not consider the use of naked lights even though Nixon expressed his belief that this would be the first of a series of accidents in the Aberdare Valley.'

Within two years Nixon's prophetic foreboding had come true. Fifty-two men perished at the Lletty Shenkin Colliery, where Edward worked. Poor Jane. When this happened, she was about to give birth to their seventh child and her dissipated energies were now accompanied by a lingering sense of chill. Eighteen months later, Jane's worst fears were realised when Edward, along with two others, lost his life in the bowels of Letty Shenkin. He was forty-three.

The accident happened on the 10th August 1849. As only three men died, it was hardly considered to be a major tragedy and therefore not well recorded. However, a piece from the book entitled *South Wales Coalmines, 1840-71,* paints a descriptive picture of the situation:-

> 'Whilst some ironmasters had put their mines in charge of competent engineers, most overmen were ignorant. The dangerous state of the Lletty Shenkin Colliery has been attributed to the lack of confidence in the overman. This was John Johns, an illiterate man of little experience: quite incompetent to be entrusted with the charge of 180 lives in one of the most dangerous collieries in Wales. Johns gave orders for a collier to work away a pillar of coal from which gas was escaping. This led to an explosion in which three men were killed and fifteen burned.'

Llewelyn Llewelyn, Edward and Jane's second son, was nine when he lost his father. He was a bright and observant child who'd noted his parents exhaustion as their long day drew to a close and seen a weariness still etched in their faces as the new one began. He'd listened silently to the rumblings of discontent within the mining community and he'd watched. He'd watched the ironmasters, the managers and their ilk, leave comfortable, well-lit houses in carriages, the occupants snugly dressed with tippets of fur to keep out the chill. These were the people who could afford servants, grooms and gardeners, whose children would be educated. These were the people who never went hungry.

"One day," said the youngster to himself, "I will have my own colliery."

When he told his mother of his thoughts, she smiled a dull smile - he was after all still a boy, so let him have his dreams. But a boy is unencumbered by the reasoning of an adult and dreams are only there to be turned into reality, and whilst others played Llewelyn studied, quickly learning to read and write. As a collier's son, he was unable to escape a stretch in the mines, but his brilliant mind and tenacity to succeed, apparent so early, ensured it would only be brief. By the time he was twenty-five, he'd become a qualified surveyor for the Powell Duffryn Collieries, with his own house in Mountain Ash. For many, this position would have been sufficient reward. For Llewelyn, it was just the beginning.

His marriage to Jane Wilkinson in 1869, when he was nearly thirty, carried him up a few more rungs of the industrial ladder. Jane came from a comfortable mining family in Sunderland and together, she and Llewelyn could afford a good standard of living with nannies to care for their seven sons and one daughter, all born within eleven years. If one is to judge by reading Llewelyn's diaries, softly bound in green leather, this feat of fatherhood must have been something of a miracle, for he was hardly ever at home. In a slanting script of faded ink, the pages are meticulously filled with details on meetings, costs and working engagements, both in this country and abroad. A one line appendage to a full page in 1877, briefly refers to his fifth son: 'At 3.00 p.m. baby baptized - Tudor.' There are no other details. Unfortunately, the little boy mentioned, lost his life at an early age due to a sporting accident at school.

Llewelyn's upwardly successful career continued unabated until he was around fifty. This included a profitable spell in Chile as a mineral adviser to the Chilean Government and a lucrative appointment as General Manager of the Powell Duffryn Company. Now he was in the midst of purchasing the Abersychan Collieries in Monmouthshire - after forty years he was about to achieve his youthful ambition. It proved to be a profitable and successful venture, yet if you go through his diaries once more, it appears that his greatest pleasure occurred when accepting the invitation to become High Sheriff of Monmouthshire, a few years before his death in 1916. Llewelyn outlived Jane by three years. His obituary makes long and impressive reading. The executor's account of the estate is even more impressive. The humble collier's boy, who set out to capture a rainbow, left £327,000 - by today's values a self-made millionaire.

Desmond's Grandfather, Llewlyn Llewelyn, High Sheriff of Monmouthshire (2nd from right)

The beneficiaries of Llewelyn's will were his only daughter, Elenita, and six remaining sons, Ernest, Herbert, Leonard, Ivor, Frank and Hedley. With such an influential father, it was only to be expected that his sons would secure managerial positions in Welsh industry with comparative ease. With the exception of Hedley, they did, but only after a stint as colliers. Llewelyn had been determined they should start where he started, at the bottom.

Hedley and Elenita were the youngest of the family, there being little more than a year between them. Both were born in Chile during the period Llewelyn had worked for the Chilean Government. Their early childhood in a foreign country differed noticeably to that of the elder brothers and perhaps this explains Hedley's colourful personality, so out of keeping with the other siblings. As he grew up, his good looks and roguish smile quickly earned him the reputation of a playboy and, having decided neither Wales nor work were his scene, he took his charms to London where he reputedly tried his luck at gambling. His inheritance represented a glorious windfall, not necessarily to be spent wisely.

Out of all Llewelyn's siblings, only Leonard, his third son, inherited his ambitious drive and inexhaustible energy. In industry, it was he who perpetuated the family name, eventually becoming recognised as one of the most accomplished mining engineers of the day and gaining a knighthood for his services to the country. By all accounts, Leonard may have been something of a snob, keen to be seen with influential people, including his friend, the politician Lloyd George. However, unlike his father who enjoyed widespread popularity in the Welsh coalfields, he had the reputation of being 'a bit of a bastard'. This bullish attitude manifested itself at an early age when he was expelled from school, supposedly for beating up the headmaster. The other brothers, Ernest, Herbert, Ivor and Frank, appeared almost dull beside him and may, apart from Ivor, have had little in common as they reached adulthood.

Ivor, tall and bespectacled with a bookish air, remained close to Leonard throughout - he also shared his passion for fast expensive cars. Otherwise, this retiring brother, with strict Victorian principles, neither wanted nor needed the glory Leonard desired. Instead, he ran his colliery at Risca with a quiet efficiency and could honestly claim to have never had a strike in his pit. His natural shyness made him ill at ease with women and relationships were few, except with his cousin, Mia Wilkinson.

Family gatherings brought Ivor and Mia together whilst still under the watchful eyes of nannies. This early friendship developed into love, certainly on Ivor's part, in their teenage years. Whether it was reciprocated in quite the same way is uncertain, as Mia remained something of a chameleon. What went on behind her dark eyes and wistful expression, neither family nor friends could ever quite fathom. The few who still remember, say her outward personality was the stronger of the two. She valued her independence and liked to hunt, play tennis and skate - the latter learned whilst at a finishing school in Switzerland. A gifted pianist since childhood, she'd spend several hours each day at the piano, although this was later displaced when she became addicted to Bridge. The admirers were many, but their offers of marriage were declined until she accepted Ivor's hesitant proposal. He was thirty-six and Mia thirty.

Their wedding took place at Risca, on 2nd September 1911. The day was fair and the sun glanced on the church decorated with lilies as the bride was escorted to the altar by her brother-in-law, Charles-de-Courcoy Parry. He then handed over the responsibility of giving her away to her mother, Mrs. Wilkinson.

How absorbing it would have been to stealthily scan the pages of Mia's diaries and discover the innermost thoughts of this enigmatic and attractive woman on such an important day. Unfortunately, these slim volumes were destroyed by her daughter more than twenty years ago and Mia's secrets have been relegated to charred embers. Instead, a factual report from the free press of Monmouthshire must suffice. The coverage is outrageously full of insignificant detail, such as the name of every wedding guest and the entire list of wedding presents, including a tea cosy and handkerchief from a Mrs. Hedley. The rest reads like a fashion page:-

> 'The bride looked charming in a Liberty satin gown, veiled with embroidered ninon and trimmed with satin cord. The skirt being elaborately designed with cord embroidery and the bodice matched accordingly; the other side arranged as a fischu trimmed with orange blossom. The yoke and the lower sleeves were of silk tuscan net and the satin train trimmed with a lover's knot composed of ninon roses and orange blossom. The bride wore a diamond and pearl necklet, the gift of the bridegroom and carried a sheath of choice lilies.'

The piece continues in the same vein with an account of the bridesmaids' dresses and the bride's mother's attire who alarmingly is described as being 'handsomely clad in bright purple velvet'. This final paragraph concludes the event:-

> 'The wedding breakfast was served at Risca House, after which the bride and bridegroom left on a tour through Ireland. The bride's travelling dress was a tailor-made costume of emerald green box cloth and she wore a motor bonnet of the same shade.'

- 2 -

FRAGMENTS OF A WELSH CHILDHOOD

Blaen-y-pant

"Whenever I dream of being a child again,
I'm always at Blaen-y-pant, on the terrace
and Nanny is calling me ..."

- 2 -
FRAGMENTS OF A WELSH CHILDHOOD

After their marriage, Ivor and Mia moved into Glenariffe, a pleasant house in the tree-lined residential suburb of Newport. Mia's own activities, both social and sporting, continued unabated and appeared entirely unaffected by having a husband and home. Together, she and Ivor played golf, indulged in their love of expensive cars (Mia was one of the first women in Wales to hold a driving licence) and holidayed in Europe. Almost three years to the day, on 12th September 1914, Mia gave birth to their first child, a son, Desmond Wilkinson.

Their lifestyle looked set to change as his vociferous cries rang through the house, insisting his parents' attention should now be firmly focused on him. Even the wet nurse, hired to relieve Mia from the rigours of breast feeding, did little to alleviate the situation. A nanny must be found immediately. Within a few days, Elizabeth Mary Jones, tiny, pretty and thirty had filled the position.

*

1915. White clouds moved gently across the sky. Could they have been smoke? Perhaps. I reached for them, chubby arms outstretched, but failed to capture the merest wisp and instead cried in frustration. A soothing voice and soft arms, smelling of soap, scooped me up. A warm, familiar smell and as I buried my head amongst the grey folds of material, hushed nothings were murmured in my ear. Dearest Nanny, mine for fifty years and nobody ever replaced you.

Nanny and her young charge, Desmond

I have vague impressions of being propped up amongst a froth of pillows, then with nanny at the helm of the pram, being taken at a spanking pace along the pavements of Newport. We must have gone to a park of some sort; trees and bright splashes of organised flowers are stored like Van Goghs, side by side, in the memory bank. There was a voice too; a man's voice and as Nanny sat on the seat, he sat beside her. They were laughing and when she put her arm through his, he smiled and you could tell she'd forgotten all about me. He wore a blue uniform. Suddenly, he didn't turn up any more and Nanny sat on the seat alone.

*

Within a year, Ivor and Mia had moved from Glenariffe to the countryside near Malpas, three miles from the dust and disturbances of Newport.

Blaen-y-pant was a substantial property, built of yellowed brick around 1880. It lay amongst several acres of undulating grounds and the long sash windows looked down

Ivor's 'Rolls'. Mia at the wheel with Ivor next to her and their chauffeur relegated to a back seat driver

Bentley No. 3. Modified for Ivor to incorporate a dicky seat

a winding driveway to the pretty gardens. Inherited with these, came an awesomely strict gardener and Mia, who loved gardening, did so at her peril.

Ivor and Mia adored Blaen-y-pant from the outset. It suited all their requirements to perfection and, most importantly, there was ample stabling for Mia's growing number of horses and garaging for Ivor's collection of sumptuous cars. Conservatories, with a promise of grapes from a knotted vine, spread out like two silver wings from the high-ceilinged rooms on the ground floor. Here, Mia could and would indulge in her love of furnishing in the heavy Victorian style of patterned papers, plants, drapes and clutter. The kitchens, scullery and, by comparison, smaller rooms at the top of the house, would naturally be the servants domain. Yet most of the action (and noise) was set to echo from the first floor, where, surrounded by a few king-sized bedrooms and a couple of bathrooms, lay the day nursery and the night nursery the hub of Desmond's childhood. This was where, twenty four hours a day, Nanny ministered to the needs of her cherubic charge, whose mass of curls and petulant expression gave him the appearance of a pretty girl.

*

1916. Different house, different rooms and different shadows. It's dark and I need the light on to chase away imaginary ghosts. Lawns spread out in front of me and as I run across them Nanny tries to catch me - not difficult when you've only just learned to walk. Wet black noses and the muddy paws of Jim and Rags push playfully against me. I fall. Nanny hauls me to my feet. "Up you come, there's a brave boy" and we go inside for tea before climbing the stairs to bed. Had to avoid the third stair at all costs, but can't remember why. We reach the nursery and have prayers with Mummie and Daddie. I remember the huge cupboards were filled with my toys and I could move the bottom shelf and climb inside. The dogs (real ones) would join me along with teddy bear and golliwog.

*

Mia's burgeoning waistline and the veiled whispers of adults did little to prepare Desmond for the shock of finding that, after three years, he suddenly had to share his beloved nanny with a baby sister. His wails, tears and repeated requests that she be taken away at once, were disregarded and Nanny, his lovely Nanny, got cross with him. Baby Noreen was here to stay and the sooner he got used to it the better. Feeling thoroughly displaced, he sought solace with his friends in the toy cupboard. Eventually his father found him red-eyed and disconsolate.

*

Ivor with Desmond, aged 3

1917. It was hot sitting in the toy cupboard. When Daddie found me, he smilingly suggested we went down to his study for a little talk. Misery forgotten. To be asked into his study made me feel very grown-up and privileged. Did we talk? If so, nothing much stuck in my mind. The rare collection of birds' eggs he showed me were far more interesting. Shelves and shelves of them; pale speckled things lying in rather dirty cotton wool. He let me touch them gently and then, for some reason, I blew on them and the effect of the dust rising in the air was enormously pleasing. Faded pieces of card were propped by each egg. Daddie picked one of these up and told me what I thought was a pretty stupid story, of an egg turning into a lovely bird and flying away. There were butterflies, stilled by a pin, side by side in glass cases.

We had biscuits and orange juice before going upstairs to say goodnight to Mummie. As she was holding 'that baby', I had to kiss 'her' goodnight, too. But none of this mattered, for when we reached the nursery, there was Nanny, her arms outstretched and smiling again.

*

Once they've risen to unsteady legs, little sisters have an infuriating way of attaching themselves to older brothers and following in their shadow. Noreen was no exception and Desmond soon grew fond of this podgy little figure trailing in his wake. Before long they became inseparable and learned to use Nanny's divided attention to their advantage.

The upbringing of the two children was almost entirely Elizabeth's responsibility and her own personal life appeared non-existent. To Desmond and Noreen, she represented the pinnacle of their world and their parents were shadowy figures, seen for an hour or so at tea-time.

*

1918. I must have been a horrendous child. Poor Nanny only had one afternoon off each week and once, when she decided to go to the pictures with a friend, I created havoc by screaming incessantly the minute she was out of sight. Blotchy, tearful and gasping for breath, my performance proved to be impressive. As my parents were convinced I was going to have a fit and die, my father frantically phoned the cinema in Newport to have an announcement flashed across the screen. 'Will Nanny Jones please return home to Blaen-y-pant where her young charge is distraught.'

On another occasion, I disappeared down the coal hole, primarily because I liked digging and this seemed to be a sensible place to fulfill this desire. Perhaps it would have been better if Noreen hadn't followed me. But we were happy (and dirty) down there, when Nanny spoiled it by turfing us out and muttering crossly that we'd quite ruined her afternoon off, as she'd had to spend most of it searching for us.

*

For both adults and children, the days at Blaen-y-pant followed a well-trodden routine, with Ivor immersed in his colliery and cars; Mia in her horses. In the mornings, Nanny endeavoured to teach her charges the simplest elements of the three R's by reading Peter Rabbit, then making them recite a passage or two from memory. In the afternoons, she took them for a walk, a ride in the pony and trap or to tea with friends. At week-ends, particularly on Sundays after church, there could be a visit from relatives. Otherwise, Ivor and Mia entertained very little and if they did, the children were not involved a great deal.

*

1919. We used to go out in the pony and trap two or three times a week. If it were quite far, Allan the groom took the reins, on short distances Nanny took command. The trap was my favourite and Nanny, fed up with my continuous nagging and anxious glances at the rain beating solidly on the windows, would say in exasperation, "I've told you before, it all depends on the weather." For Nanny, it always 'depended'. Even if it were brilliant sunshine and eighty degrees, blankets and brollies would be taken 'just in case'. A comfort to her constant fretting over Noreen and I catching a chill.

On Mondays we had tea with the Laybournes. On Thursday (or was it Friday) they came to us. Their gargantuan affair, I preferred to our daintier version, chiefly because

Desmond and his sister, Noreen

old Mrs. Laybourne made wonderful rhubarb jam, pink and filled with stringy bits of rhubarb. We slurped great dollops of it from doorstep slices of fresh bread. But, if Mrs. L noticed somebody taking buttered bread, then on no account would she allow you to have any of her jam.

Richard Laybourne must have been about my age. Surrounded by a gaggle of six sisters, we grew up together as our parents had been friends for years. We were to remain close throughout his life, cut tragically short by a flying accident in 1938, a few weeks before he was due to be best man at my wedding.

*

As with many children, their private world of make believe and disguise is real and very important. This applied to Desmond and, apart from one or two lapses, it never really showed any signs of abating. As a child, he spent many hours lurking amongst the dark corners of Blaen-y-pant impersonating a king, cardinal or rogue about to fight for, and save, a fair maid (usually an acquiescent Noreen) from disaster. Friends were often cajoled into participating in the various charades, but not necessarily willingly. They got a trifle fed up, because he insisted on having the best role, leaving them to rot in dungeons or perish under the hand of a swash buckling pirate. Should this latent young actor have the chance to dress up and perform in front of a real live audience - never mind if it were only Nanny and a couple of dogs, bribed with biscuits to sit still- he'd jump at it. Perhaps this was why the razzmatazz of the hospital ball, a yearly charity event for children, proved to be such an attraction for him.

*

1920. I loved prinking around in fancy dress. The first time my parents took me I was three and went as a Scottish soldier, bedecked in frills and a kilt. Unfortunately, nobody bothered to cut my hair and I was mistaken for a girl. Happily there were other years, other balls and other outfits for them to rectify this unfortunate mistake: a black and white ensemble and I became a jester: heavy clogs and a short jacket - a Dutch boy: the unmistakable blue garb of a sailor and, curiously, one year they transformed me into an impecunious child clad in patched trews, heavy boots and a cloth cap, resembling the less fortunate offspring of a coal miner.

A bicycle, gloriously shiny and new, arrived on my sixth birthday. A gift from Uncle Leonard, an extremely generous man. Because of his unbounding generosity, he rated as the favourite uncle. By comparison, the rest, including poor old Uncle Frank (my godfather), sank to the bottom of my esteem, due entirely and unfairly, to the quality of their presents.

Starting school coincided with my sixth birthday. I'd report at 9.00 a.m. sharp to Miss James in Newport, who used her home as the premises for teaching pre-prep school monsters a bit of sense. The morning only curriculum probably meant she'd had enough by lunch-time. My father, not my mother, always drove me to school and picked me up again at 12.30 p.m. This blissfully happy experience made me foolishly assume my entire schooldays would run along these lines.

*

Horses were undoubtedly Mia's first love and four of these magnificent creatures were an integral part of the scene at Blaen-y-pant. To this day, Desmond swears his mother gave him a bit, not a teething ring to chew on. However, from her, he and Noreen inherited a great affection not only for horses, but for all animals and at Mia's insistence, each had their own pony and learned to ride at an early age.

By contrast, Ivor had little or nothing to do with horses and rarely visited the stables. As Desmond cannot recollect ever seeing him on horseback, it's possible he never learned to ride and found these wilful animals rather awesome. Nor does Ivor feature in any of the many horsey photographs. These faded brown things, torn at the edges, show Mia, elegant on Falcon, wearing a dark habit and riding side-saddle, about to go hunting with the local Llangibby and Tredegar Hounds. Mia caught unawares, windblown and laughing on her favourite 'Cumalong'. Mia standing self consciously between her four horses, arms outstretched and hands cupped under their whiskery chins. Several snaps, this time of Desmond, grinning uncertainly from Nutty's broad back. Others of Noreen on Daisy - of the two, more at ease with her mount.

*

1921. Nutty was a sturdy little thing whose colouring fell somewhere between a pickled walnut and a ripe conker. He could be damned difficult and took great delight in bucking to rid himself of any encumbrance. Consequently, I was always falling off, but got no sympathy. All a part of the learning process.

It's odd because, although my mother was a brilliant horsewoman, she never involved herself in teaching us to ride. Instead, she left it all to Allan whose methods were horribly basic. Like some Commanding Officer, he'd issue instructions in a loud voice. 'You look like a sack of potatoes.' 'Knees in.' 'Heels down.' 'Back straight.' At the slightest mistake, he'd flip his whip across my wrists, which stung like hell. Looking back, his tough form of tuition (Noreen suffered it too) stood me in good stead, particularly when I auditioned for Follyfoot in the 1970's.

*

Mia with her two children and stable of horses

More photos, tantalising glimpses of forgotten friends, once so close, gaze expectantly from the pages of worn albums. Dogs, not horses, suddenly feature: Pip and Bimbo reclining in separate wheelbarrows pushed across the lawn by Desmond and Noreen: Bonzo at the seaside held by Ivor. Captain, Rupert and Pip again, enjoying the attentions of the family at their holiday home at Ogmore-by-sea, situated some forty miles west of Newport.

Ivor and Mia first purchased a small cottage at Ogmore-by-Sea in 1917, realising almost instantly that the tiny rooms would be inadequate. When Sandymount, an ideally large but unexciting Edwardian house became available, they lost no time in buying. It commanded an enviable position, with the gardens fronting onto a sandy stretch of heathland before reaching a wide expanse of the seashore. For Ivor and Mia, whose interests were diverse, the property had an even greater asset as it lay in very close proximity to Southerndown, a well known golf course encapsulated in the rolling coastal scenery.

Each June, July and August, Sandymount became the Llewelyn's summer residence and Blaen-y-pant grew silent and deserted. The groom, who doubled as a chauffeur, provided the link between the two. It's unclear whether Ivor went back to work at any point during this lengthy vacation. Desmond doesn't think so, but three months seems rather a long time for a manager to be absent from his workplace, particularly as the Risca collieries were only about thirty miles away.

Inexplicably, neither Ivor nor Mia ever visited Sandymount 'out of season' and again one cannot help but feel a certain curiosity, for both loved driving and undertook far longer journeys when visiting friends or relatives just for the day. As neither time nor money could be considered a problem, one must lay the reason with the vagaries of a different era.

*

1922. Ogmore, Sandymount, Southerdown, one Utopia wrapped in blue sky. Surely it must have rained at some point during those summer months. If so I don't remember. To me the sun always shone, grown-ups wore carefree personalities and Noreen and I had rather special summer friends from the neighbouring holiday cottages. Did my parents laugh and talk more? It seemed so and unlike Blaen-y-pant, we had a constant stream of visitors at Sandymount. Even Uncle Hedley wrenched himself away from the attractions of London to spend a few days with us, claiming the rest would do him good. Obviously, he must have been an absolute old roue, but he fascinated me. Particularly as Nanny felt he'd be a bad influence and insisted I should neither believe nor preferably even listen to his tales, which were always told accompanied by a glass of whiskey.

Cousins Nina and Hope often visited. Hope was my age, a plain gawky child whose subsequent transformation into a teenage beauty left me totally besotted. Unfortunately, I was too scared to try anything other than necking.

Although my parents played golf a great deal, my father still found time to come to the beach and join us for a swim. Nanny always wore a hideous black woolly thing in the sea and my father used to tease her, but I'm pretty certain they both had a very soft spot for each other. My mother hated swimming and played tennis instead.

Picnic lunches, or lack of them, were my greatest disappointment of the holidays. For some unknown reason we could have a picnic tea, but not lunch. At 12.30, we'd troop back to Sandymount for a proper sit down affair indoors. How I envied those friends lucky enough to rush straight from the sea and, flinging a towel around chilly shoulders, would wriggle wet backsides to make a comfortable seat in the sand and eat sandwiches with gritty fingers."

*

Growing up can be a hurtful business and the question of 'Where shall we send Desmond to school?' caused Ivor and Mia a fair amount of concern. For the nine year old Desmond, who initially found the idea of boarding school intriguing, it spelled the uncertain beginnings of a new chapter. After much dithering, the choice eventually fell on The Priory, a prep boarding school in Malvern.

Preparations for the unknown appeared exciting. Trying on the school uniform, adding the cap and pulling faces at the mirror simply resembled dressing-up for another charade, fun, but not for real. Even the pristine white shirts and pile of socks held a perverse thrill, dampened only by Nanny's complaints, because she had to sew name tags in everything. The suspense reached its height when the trunks arrived with the name Desmond W. Llewelyn importantly emblazoned across the top.

Exactly one week before he was due to start school, Ivor took his young son to the barbers in Newport and within a few minutes his curly locks had fallen to the floor. Nanny's darling boy was growing up at last.

*

1923. It was in the lavatory, a couple of days later, when the 'leaving home terror' suddenly hit me. Sitting in that tiny room, where everything was so safe and familiar, I panicked and thought this time next week I'll be sitting on a strange lavatory - a weird, scary feeling. From that moment, I mentally started saying goodbye to my favourite objects; a train set, a rocking horse, my bicycle and so on. Feeling progressively worse, I also wished the nursery, the lavatory and the third stair (from the top) farewell too.

Just three more days at Blaen-y-pant. I pleaded desperately, first with my father, then with my mother, not to send me away to boarding school. In turn they refused. I suggested a tutor: the Laybournes had tutors, why not me? They refused again. The minutes continued to tick relentlessly away and I feigned illness. In fact, I did indeed feel sick, sicker than I'd ever felt before. But to no avail. When the day of departure dawned, I buried my face in Nutty's warm brown mane and kissed him goodbye. Twelve weeks seemed like eternity.

The groom loaded the car with my trunks and odd bags. The seats smelled of wax as I opened the door and climbed in beside my father, who'd been waiting at the wheel to drive me to Malvern. My mother, Noreen and Nanny, darling Nanny, her white collar awry and tears in her eyes, stood outside Blaen-y-pant and waved goodbye. I felt utterly, utterly desolate and remained silent for most of the journey. On reaching Malvern, we went into The Priory and I met Mr. Allen, my new headmaster for the first time. He smiled, shook my hand and said, "I'm sure you'll like it here." I knew better. That night, my lonely fitful sleep and damp pillow were accompanied by the noise of a snivelling dormitory.

*

The inaugural miseries of boarding school subsided as Desmond's pragmatic outlook accepted the inevitable and adjusted to a new environment. The Priory, a lovely old, but inconvenient building (now the Council Offices), housed about 70 pupils and was in a sad state of disrepair. Within a year, Mr. Giles and Mr. Allen, joint headmasters, had moved the school to a new premises, the Wood Norton Estate at Fladbury, about 18 miles from Malvern. This rather grand property once belonged to the Duke of Orleans and the great gates guarding the entrance were supposedly replicas of those at Versailles. Amongst the remnants of tended grounds lay a lake, used by the boys for skating on wintry days, a ruined chapel and overgrown bear pits, later converted into swimming baths.

All this, plus the fact that Auntie Gwen and Uncle Charlie (his mother's sister and brother-in-law) lived in Malvern, provided Desmond with some palatable distractions from the tedium of schoolwork. It also helped fill the void caused by the enforced absence from Blaen-y-pant.

*

1924. I missed Nanny more than anything. She wrote, of course, and so did my parents, but only occasionally. Thank God for Auntie Gwen and Uncle Charlie who were very long suffering. When The Priory was in Malvern, I used to see them most weekends; at Wood Norton, distance rendered them less accessible. Instead, Uncle Charlie used to fetch me after church on Sundays and, with a suppressed sigh of relief, drive me back in the evenings.

I vividly recall the day when a classmate sidled up to me in prep and muttered,"You any relation to Sir Leonard Llewelyn?" "Yes," I replied, somewhat warily. "He's my uncle - so?" "Well, the papers say he's dead," said the boy (whose name escapes me) in the smug whisper of one-up-manship. Nobody, not even Nanny, wrote to tell me my favourite Uncle had died of a heart attack at fifty. My parents never mentioned his death, nor the funeral, and obviously thought it unnecessary for me to attend.

*

In spite of a strict regime and masters who, if they felt so inclined, pulled hair, twisted ears or caned the boys backsides, Desmond enjoyed his prep school. At the beginning of each term, he briefly wallowed in the sorrows of leaving home, but this quickly evaporated as friendships were renewed and the general curriculum of doing as little as possible without getting punished got under way.

It's questionable whether Desmond's lack of learning ability can be blamed on the teachers being, in his words, "Shell shocked soldiers not academics" or the fact that he was basically idle and preferred the freedom of an outdoor life.

Sport of any kind, he excelled at and now, on the yearly vacation to Sandymount, he rose at dawn and spent much of his time working at the local farm. Here, the farmer's son, Cornelius, educated his eager young helper in the elementary aspects of farming; the first being milking and the twice daily milk round, delivered at a leisurely pace from a horse drawn float.

*

1925. At eleven or twelve I seriously considered being a farmer. My father had tut-tutted against any childish dreams of acting, claiming this profession was 'filled with queers and loose women'. I wasn't sure what he meant, but it sounded interesting. It occurred to me later, these conclusions were only based on his Victorian attitude, for apart from one or two pantomimes, he never set foot in the theatre. My mother took me a few times and I recollect seeing Paul Robeson in Showboat *and the legendary Anna Pavlova dance. My father, however, adored rugby and we went to many rugby matches together. Like most other schoolboys, my ambition (unfulfilled) was to play for Wales.*

*

One of the strange aspects of Desmond's youth was his complete and utter oblivion to the poverty and appalling working conditions in the Welsh mining villages. Nor did he ever become aware of the antipathy felt by the miners towards their employers and families. Being spat at by the local children, or having to avoid the rougher parts of Newport were, to Desmond, a mild nuisance, best ignored and left unquestioned.

Perhaps the blame (if it is blame) has to be attributed to Ivor and Mia, who seemed overly anxious to keep their offspring protected from anything other than the joys of the formative years. This attitude to the less agreeable situations of life probably also explains why both Desmond and Noreen were only vaguely aware of the deterioration of their father's health.

The medical records indicate various heart problems within the Llewelyn family and Ivor's angina, which today would have been alleviated with a few pills, in the twenties necessitated constant rest and keeping warm. Luckily, Blaen-y-pant had central heating.

"The house was kept at greenhouse temperature except on the hottest summer days, when father would sit in a wheelchair in the garden."

Because of his disability, Ivor was forced to retire from the colliery in 1924, but found his semi-invalid state rather dull and, possibly, to relieve the tedium, dabbled in shares. Initially, Ivor did well. Latterly, maybe due to ill-advice, his investments proved unwise. The Bingo goldmines and solid wheeled bicycles were just two examples of misguided buying. On good days, he still played golf for a couple of hours and participated in the family holidays. Driving his beloved Bentley remained an indulgence entirely unaffected by his health and he regularly made long trips, including fetching and carrying his son from school.

In 1927, Desmond left The Priory, but his lax approach to schoolwork had finally caught up with him. This necessitated several months extra coaching before being able to pass the entrance exam to Radley College. With half a dozen other boys, he went to Southminster in Essex, where the brilliant, but strange tutor, questioned his pupils almost daily about their masturbation habits as well as their school work. "He was a curious little man with the habit of coming into dormitory and flinging back the bed clothes to see if we had been playing with ourselves."

Radley College, Desmond's next educational port lies near Oxford amongst the rolling parkland set out by Capability Brown. Since those early days, when it was known as Radley Hall, it has probably grown tenfold.

Built around the 1720's by a Sir John Stonehouse, the property remained in the family until his great grandson became the occupier. This gentleman had a partiality for good living but lacked sufficient funds to accommodate it. His entrepreneurial instincts were poor and after several abortive business ventures, denuded Radley of its contents and went to try his luck abroad; his inheritance he left rented out as a school. This too proved unsuccessful and the empty building and surrounding grounds became neglected and overgrown.

The sorry plight of Radley Hall was brought to the attention of a William Sewell, who surveyed the property on 8th March 1847. He pronounced it to be exactly the right place to set up his visionary school for 'Christian young gentlemen' within easy reach of London.

Radley's problems were over; William Sewell's had just started. Seemingly undeterred by the ghostly tales and Radley's previous failure as a school, Sewell set about negotiating the tenure and raising the not inconsiderable amount of cash needed for restoration and furnishing; most of which he begged or borrowed.

Remarkably, Sewell's optimistic character and influential friendships bore fruit with surprising speed. By September 1847, Radley, once again bulging with antiques, stained glass and paintings, received its first pupils. According to Christopher Hibbert's excellent history of Radley College entitled *'No Ordinary Place'*, the pupils numbered just two or three. However, by January 1848, this had swollen to ten, rising to fifty the next year.

By the time the fourteen year old D.W. Llewelyn put an apprehensive foot across the threshold, over three hundred gowned pupils were entrenched in the Radley system.

*

1928. I was down for Harrow, the school supposedly tagged for rich men's sons. Purely by chance, my mother fell into conversation with a master from Radley at a party. He must have flattered her considerably because, by the end of the evening, she'd switched her allegiance from Harrow.

Having been pre-conditioned by a fairly tough prep school, I discovered life at Radley unexpectedly more relaxed. I even grew accustomed to the outdated ritual of a daily cold bath, particularly as shirking this freezing routine earned a beating from the Prefects.

Looking back, I was probably a bit thick and after a term in the bottom form, went on to stay in the next one for over two years. Although this may have reflected some of the poor standards of teaching.

*

Tall, gangly and academically mediocre, Desmond refers to Radley as, "Where I spent some of my happiest days."

To him, those selfish days of youth meant nothing mattered but rugger and the theatre. Initially, rugger took over to such an extent that his classmates dubbed him 'loopy Llewelyn'.

*

1929. My somewhat dodgy rugger tactics were partially gleaned from watching Newport. However, secret hopes of some day playing for Wales were dashed when Guy Morgan (a former Rugby international), joined Radley as a master. After one glorious scrum he tapped me on the shoulder.

"What's your name?"

"Llewelyn Sir," I replied.

"Well, cut it out Llewelyn. I'm a Welshman, too, and I know all their dirty tricks."

Guy and his wife became close friends and years later, as a tutor, crippled with arthritis and no longer able to even limp round the field, my son, Ivor, went into his Social.

Having watched the production 'R.U.R.', *I joined the Amateur Dramatic Society at Radley to build scenery and restore the stage. It was Dennis Price, my study mate, who persuaded me to act instead and we appeared together in* Bulldog Drummond, *followed by* Escape *and* She Stoops to Conquer. *The sweet, heady applause removed the need for further persuasion and I became so hooked on Amateur Dramatics that rugger slipped into second place. We even performed some of the plays at St. Peter's, London Docks, where, accompanied by the sweet smell of spices exuding from the warehouses, I learned all the rituals of the Anglican Church as well.*

*

Both socially and structurally, Radley had begun undergoing changes. The number of pupils was increasing and buildings needed modernizing, extending, and the antiquated facilities renewing. Outdated rules had to be re-hashed. The teaching

'Growing up'

methods, or lack of them, came in for criticism by visiting inspectors. Christopher Hibbert reckons that although generally they professed to find the standard of teaching adequate, their reports were littered with comments similar to: 'a monotonous teacher of an interesting subject'; 'problems with discipline'; or, 'ruled by pupils'; 'inexperienced and sleepy'. Raised fees, now 185 guineas a year (£194.25) went towards refurbishment and better education with more up-to-date methods.

Claimed as successful, the changes appeared to have little effect on Desmond, whose termly reports, apart from drama, rugby and history, showed little improvement.

*

1930. The joy of a golden October turned a cold dreary grey when I was told by the social tutor that my father had died. Just like that. No inklings or warnings had heralded his sudden departure from life at fifty-five. I remember him calling me into his study and wondering why he looked so ill at ease, little knowing my mother had committed the wretched task of informing me about my father's demise to this poor teacher. He asked me to sit down and cleared his throat before saying, "Unfortunately Llewelyn, I have some very sad news. Your father died yesterday from a heart attack."

Feelings of disbelief, anger, misery and sadness gave way to tears. I blubbered loudly and wildly and the hapless man looked even more uncomfortable. "Pull yourself together Llewelyn. Have a few hours off - might help." I did, but not before returning to his study again. "Please sir, did my mother say when I should leave for the funeral?" "Your mother" he replied, in a voice unlike his own,"feels it totally unnecessary for you to take time off school to attend your father's funeral."

The Uncle Leonard situation all over again, but a thousand times worse and I was left unhappily, alone.

*

Far from Ivor's death being a dignified exit, leaving a widow and two children to grieve together, it widened channels and disclosed a nest of unsavoury circumstances, hitherto unforseen.

*

1931. Having had no direct communication with my mother or Nanny since my father's death, I returned to Blaen-y-pant for the Christmas holidays with some trepidation.

Within seconds, I realised the Blaen-y-pant I knew had vanished for ever. It lacked warmth both in spirit and temperature. One miserable fire flickered in the sitting room grate, curtains remained drawn, perhaps to stop the modicum of heat from escaping. Vases stood emptily, unadorned by flowers. Even the plants had curled and dried into grotesque postures. My mother, upright, dressed in black and looking oddly vulnerable, remained uncommunicative and refused to mention my father's name.

It transpired that my father had died unexpectedly and, apart from Nanny, alone whilst my mother was out playing Bridge. She seemed unable to forgive herself for this, although he'd showed no symptoms of illness before she left. An almost worse shock followed when the solicitors disclosed the disastrous state of Ivor's financial affairs. His debts of over £30,000, the net results of his heedless gambling on the share market, left us almost completely bankrupt and as the creditors stood with their hands outstretched (not literally), Blaen-y-pant would have to be sold. Some years later, I learned that my father had used all my mother's money, too - presumably with her blessing, in the hopes his luck would change.

The best bit of that year was catching the train back to Radley from Paddington Station, after the Ascension Day holiday. There, dressed in scarlet and next to her father, Gerald, stood Daphne du Maurier. With her chin up and fair hair flying, I thought she was the most beautiful creature on earth.

*

Desmond guarded his family's poverty stricken circumstances from friends and masters alike; a task made easier by Uncle Charlie taking on the responsibility for the rest of his education at Radley. For a while, Mia too kept up outward appearances, perhaps to stave off creditors, but the inevitable changes took place as the skein of Ivor's financial tangles slowly unravelled.

The servants were the first to go, then the cars and horses were sold and the groom dismissed. And before the entire contents of Blaen-y-pant, piece by piece, memory by memory, lot by lot fell under the auctioneer's hammer, the property was let furnished whilst solicitors struggled with Ivor's complicated affairs. With only Nanny to keep her company, Mia retreated to the house at Ogmore-by-Sea. Two years later Blaen-y-pant went up for sale.

*

1932. Last year at Radley. Decisions on the future. Not being an academic made it difficult. Acting? I would have liked to, but sensed my father frowning down on such a choice. Rugger? Sadly not good enough. The church? Could be a possibility; not dissimilar to acting, just a case of swopping the stage for a pulpit. A voluntary week-end retreat with the Cowley Fathers in Westminster offered a decider, except I'd just met a very pretty girl at the Hunt Ball, so I was hardly 'of holy mind'.

Nevertheless, armed with Film World *and the company of Dennis Price (also keen to explore this avenue), we set off, secretly hoping for a bit of a laugh. Hopes were dashed on arrival when we were told that this was a silent retreat.*

After a session of lengthy prayers, we were sent to sparsely furnished solitary cells to contemplate our sins; 'so good for the soul'. Non-existent sins take little contemplation and I read 'Film World' *instead. Two hours passed. More prayers and more sins needing more contemplation, but only one copy of* Film World. *Supper brought more than a blessed relief. By a stroke of misguided luck, something I ate upset me and I spent most of the night being sick. Feeling gratefully rotten, I asked to be excused from the rest of the retreat and went home, leaving poor old Dennis to suffer the silence.*

*

Having been advised extra tuition would be necessary to get the School Certificate, Desmond left Radley and spent nine months with a coach in Swanage in the hope of rectifying this scholarly blip. Not a chance. Instead he and fellow student Peter Morey, a good-looking rogue who would eventually become his brother-in-law, found attractions other than work beckoned. On an escapade to London, with Peter, Desmond experienced his first, and by his own admission, 'woefully unsuccessful' encounter with a prostitute.

*

1933. Failed abysmally - at everything.

- 3 -

THEATRICAL MEMORABILIA

"There was never a moment to spare in Repertory.
It really was damned hard work."

- 3 -
THEATRICAL MEMORABILIA

England 1936. As King Edward VIII acceded to the throne, so his affair with American divorcee, Wallis Simpson, became public property and rocked the monarchy. In Germany, the worryingly powerful figure of Adolf Hitler grew closer to home. Whilst here, Winston Churchill remained temporarily in a parliamentary wilderness. Nobody wanted another war.

Desirable ladies graced the screens and the limpid eyes of Garbo, Dietrich and the like gazed up at the rugged charms of Leslie Howard or Gary Cooper. Ginger Rogers and Fred Astaire had sung and danced their way through *Gay Divorce.* Noel Coward displayed a sophisticated indifference to his ongoing successes as an actor, writer and composer.

Ian Fleming, his rebellious reputation firmly in place, had already carved a path through Eton, Sandhurst and the Army to become one of the world's worst stockbrokers. His mental labyrinth hadn't yet conceived James Bond. At 28, Cubby Broccoli, future producer of the Bond films, had been in Hollywood a matter of months and found great difficulty in earning any money at all. Sean Connery was six.

Back home, in the valleys of South Wales, not much had changed and the mining communities still struggled against poverty and appalling conditions. Collier's son, Richard Burton, whose acting fame lay in the uncharted future, was a wild, bumptious schoolboy. In September 1936, Desmond turned twenty-two and although most aspiring actors showed a preference for London, his first job, after two years at RADA, took him to Southend-on-Sea.

Outwardly, fate had fashioned Desmond kindly; his good looks, a broad shouldered 6ft 3in stature and a craggy smile ensured a succession of pretty women clung to his arm. A gregarious personality, ready sense of humour and a naive charm kept them amused. Yet in spite of these enviable attributes, an inward insecurity made him wary of rebuff - which could have been why his physical approaches to the opposite sex were inhibited and why the majority of his relationships remained platonic. One can assume this lack of confidence was a family trait inherited from his father. Being broke didn't help either.

A note from his diary also indicates a possible selfishness: 'It seems to me if you sleep with a woman for free it's less fun than a prostitute, as you have to do all sorts of things so she enjoys it too!' Desmond admits to being selfish - and a frightful scrounger. He and his chum Peter Morey, were always strapped for cash and consequently cultivated useful girlfriends; girls that had access to cinema passes, cheap meals and anything else resembling a complimentary bonus. Scrounging even extended to lying on top of a taxi roof to get a buckshee ride. Now, after several false starts, his life looked set to change. As the bright lights of stardom twinkled in the sky, Desmond embarked on his future as an actor.

"I'd tried the church and that failed. I was too dim for accountancy, too short-sighted for the police force and an insufficient liar to make a good politician. What else was left but to become an actor? I remember Richard Burton saying to me years later that the reason there are so many Welsh actors is because the church is not very popular nowadays."

In the months prior to RADA, an actual dalliance with accountancy had indeed bored him to death. This was not surprising as he'd spent most of his trial period at the Primrose and Len Dairies in Maidstone, licking stamps. A fortunate bout of scarlet fever put an end to this dismal occupation and after a recovery period, he went to RADA in 1934.

Originally formed by Herbert Tree, The Royal Academy of Dramatic Art had dwindled into more of a glorified girl's finishing school and by the thirties was desperate for male students. So, in spite of his limping on to the stage nursing a sprained ankle and giving a rotten rendering from *Lear,* they accepted Desmond. Amongst his counterparts were Geoffrey Keen (later to work with him in Bond), Pamela Brown and Margaret Lockwood - "to whom I quite lost my heart."

By comparison to current schedules, the hours at RADA in those days resembled a series of mildly disciplined tea parties. "We learnt how to fall, cry, laugh, fence, dance and, from one old boy, voice production. Every week he'd tell us the same thing :- 'speak from your diaphragm, press here and remember - tip of tongue, teeth and lips'. Play after play had to be rehearsed and the end of term production would always be attended by the Principal. With hindsight, one learnt more starting right at the bottom of a repertory company."

Leisure hours were spent with RADA counterparts; friends whose names, except for the few, are forgotten. "Helen Christie, ah, no, she was at the Talza, but she knitted me a sweater. Douglas Beech Grant, he owned a Bentley and didn't mind who drove it and Derek Tansley - well, I still see him fairly regularly today."

May 1935. Douglas Beech Grant, Geoffrey Keen and Desmond

At his digs at 1, Haven Green, Ealing, Desmond fell under the homely ministrations of a Mr. and Mrs. Reading. For twenty-five bob (£1.25p) a week they lavished their 'boys' - the others were four burly Scotsmen - with dinner, bed and breakfast and Sunday lunch. Beer at 2 1/2d (1p) a pint provided a cheap and sociable way of passing a few hours. "It was rugger on Saturdays, and then on to a pub in

Richmond, followed by a mad rush to a club in Piccadilly before returning to Ealing for a cold supper around 1 am. Next morning we were all back in the pub by midday."

An essential luxury was a regular visit to the cinema on Sunday afternoon costing 1/6d (7p). Here, Desmond immersed himself in four solid hours of entertainment offering the main film, plus a B feature film, a Disney cartoon and a short stage show of dancers or comedians. His first suit, an outrageously checked ensemble, sported fashionable plus fours and cost £3, a gift from Mia, who also gave him a weekly allowance of the same amount. Bearing in mind her impoverished circumstances, this was extremely generous. Dressed thus and clutching RADA's Certificate of Merit together with a handful of Press cuttings on his year's final production, the fledgling considered himself to be suitably ready for launching.

An added bonus was the experience he'd gained whilst still at RADA when he appeared in the Gracie Fields film, *Look Up and Laugh,* followed by a play with the Cardiff Repertory Company. "Mrs. Basil Rathbone was in the cast and I recollect the marvellous line, 'Either he's dead or his watch has stopped.'." Disappointingly, most critics only gave Desmond, who played Henry of Navarre in *Massacre,* a cursory mention. This piece is from *The Morning Post* dated 23rd June 1936:-

> 'The students of The Royal Academy of Dramatic Art with Miss Beatrice Wilson as their Producer gave a gallant performance. Miss Helen Jeffries (Catherine), Mr. Richard Spranger, Miss Noel Gordon, Mr. John Penrose, Mr. Paul Stephenson, Miss Patsy Smart and Mr. Desmond Llewelyn all deserve a mention. Mr. John Whiting in the profoundly difficult role as King finally acquitted himself.'

Undaunted, Desmond applied for auditions in repertory and exactly four weeks later received a letter from Lodge Percy, the producer-cum-manager of the Little Theatre Company at Southend-on-Sea:-

> 'This letter will confirm our engagement of you for one month certain to commence August 10th (rehearse August 4th) at the terms of £2-10-0d per week and you agree to accept in the case of bad business such proportion of that sum as may be paid to other artists pro rata.'

Done. Desmond made his inaugural appearance at the Talza Theatre in *Distinguished Gathering* on 10th August 1936. The auditorium held around 250 and seats, unreserved at 9d (4p) and at 1/- (5p) or reserved at 1/9d (9p) and 2/6d (12p), meant that more often than not, it was half empty. If the lack of theatregoers failed to dampen his enthusiasm, he wasn't quite so keen on the

Week Commencing Monday, August 10th.

THE LITTLE THEATRE CO. Present

"DISTINGUISHED GATHERING"

By JAMES PARISH.

CHARACTERS (in order of appearance):

Felix Montague	WILLIAM PRINGLE
Judith Montague	HILDA MOSS
C. D. Williams	GEOFFREY MILES
Sir Brian Howett	DESMOND LLEWELYN
Lady Thalia Wilmer	GWEN DELMAR
Major Runty Pearson	JOHN VAIZEY
Caroline Beckwith	BLANCHE CLARKSON
Dorinda Caswell	RAY GILLMAN
Leslie Gest	HELEN CHRISTIE
Eliot Richard Vines	FREDERICK COOK
Blair	PATRICIA PRIOR
Detective Inspector Rutherford	CYRIL WYATT
Detective Sergeant Ferris	DEREK SYME

The action of the play takes place in the Montague's house, at Hampstead. There is a lapse of time of one hour between Acts I and II, and half-an-hour between Acts II. and III.

THE PLAY PRODUCED BY LODGE PERCY.

The set constructed by George Hooper.

Scenery painted by Maurice Davis.

Cigarettes by ABDULLA.

effect it had on his weekly pay packet. Nevertheless, he stayed on at the Talza Theatre and the following February, a local newspaper printed a clutch of flattering comments together with a photograph of Desmond looking extraordinarily young and vulnerable:-

> 'This charming young man has graduated from the Royal Academy of Dramatic Art where he was a brilliant finalist. He joined the Little Theatre Company last August and made an immediate impression in *Distinguished Gathering* and *Devonshire Cream*. Since then he has appeared in many and various roles with great success. He is a very versatile young man and is equally at home in serious plays as when playing the giant in a pantomime.'

After six months with Lodge Percy, Desmond grew restless. He wanted to earn more money and explore new avenues. His attitude grew a little careless and Lodge Percy lost no time in criticizing - and in front of the entire cast :- "It would be a great deal easier for everybody if Mr. Llewelyn learnt his lines instead of making them up to suit himself." Privately, Desmond didn't agree, but he liked Lodge Percy and bowed to his voice of experience.

During the 1930's, repertory companies were considered to hold the future of the English stage in their palms. Within the theatrical world, it was recognised that somewhere amongst each cast lurked the professionals destined to find their way to the West End harbouring a wealth of experience gained from repertory. It's interesting to examine the routine of such a theatre; the repetitive slog undertaken by most actors and actresses, acknowledging that this supplied the stepping stone to fame. After all, where else could one acquire such versatility, or test the powers of a phenomenal memory by playing a different character week by week, as well as learning the backstage art of production?

The whole scenario was, in Desmond's words, "damned hard work", for in that short space of seven days each player must learn a new role for next week whilst continuing to perform his/her current part each evening, plus two matinees. Therefore, the Producer, pressed for time, had to rehearse the cast for the forthcoming play during the available mornings. Meanwhile the Stage Manager or his assistant, dashed around collecting the appropriate furniture, ornaments, costumes, wigs and associated items to supplement their own meagre selection of 'props'. Bills, advertisements and programmes were bashed out on antiquated typewriters and whisked off to the printers. And when the curtain finally fell on Saturday night's show, the scenery had to be dismantled, re-vamped, re-assembled and re-painted in readiness for the new production on Monday. Even Sundays were not considered sacred; the artist would be busy with his brush; the electrician with his lighting - whilst the cast were still frantically perfecting lines for the new play.

Mondays dawned early. The Producer could, at last, stage his one and only dress rehearsal in readiness for the first performance that evening, which hopefully would pass without a hitch. Then on Tuesday, "the whole damned rigmarole began again for the next week's production."

Bearing in mind Lodge Percy staged around fifty plays a year, it was a tough routine and required a good deal of staying power from all those involved.

But the time had come to broaden horizons and a chance meeting with RADA friend, Derek Tansley, set the already gathering winds of change into motion. Derek, at present, was appearing with the Matthew Forsyth Players, a travelling repertory theatre run by Matthew Forsyth. His impressive eulogy of the company included a better salary and without hesitation, Desmond contacted the Producer and asked to be considered if any vacancies arose. Pasted to the pages of a worn scrapbook is Matthew's terse reply to Desmond's enquiries:-

> 9th March 1937
> I will see you if you come to the theatre one morning at 10 o'clock.
>
> Faithfully yours, M.F.

A handwritten letter to Desmond from the Honorary Secretary of The Little Theatre Company dated 14th March 1937 followed:-

> Further to your letter of the 11th inst. and our phone conversation of the same date, the Association accepts, with regret, your resignation from the Little Theatre Company to take effect from the 20th inst.. We are very sorry to lose your services and extend to you our best wishes for your future.

On the 27th March 1937, *The Scarlet Pimpernel* opened at the Palace Theatre, Westcliff-on-Sea. Christopher Quest played Sir Percy Blakeney, Basil Dignam, the villainous Chauvelin and Mona Washbourne, Lady Blakeney. Desmond took the part of Lord Anthony Dewhurst and friend, Derek, commandeered two roles, that of 'A Citizen' and Lord Grenville. Baroness Orczy's story ended a five week run at Westcliff and met some favourable reviews:-

> 'This ageless romantic tale, combining the excitement of a thriller, kept the Easter audience enthralled, albeit a rather heavy production (the cast numbered around forty) for such a small theatre... We all welcome the appearance of the well known actor Desmond Llewelyn from the Talza Theatre.'

If Matthew initially had hopes of grooming Desmond into a leading man, he would soon be disappointed. For some inexplicable reason, it never worked out. Maybe it was due to Desmond's odd lapses in remembering his lines. Or perhaps Matthew never gave him an opportunity to prove his full potential in a suitable role; a planned oversight that left Desmond feeling miffed and perplexed.

From Westcliff, the Forsyth Players moved on to the Pavilion Theatre in Torquay for *The Millionairess.* Here, Desmond discovered some of the ramifications of travelling actors, when he, Dennis Shand and Derek Tansley declined to book any accommodation. Digs for itinerant companies had to be cheap, provide a late night supper and an even later breakfast. Every major town offered a limited selection, but bearing in mind the number of repertory theatres in the thirties, they got booked up pretty quickly. However, these three egocentric young actors decided a hotel would be more to their liking and with bargaining in mind, walked the streets of Torquay searching for suitably priced accommodation. They finally settled on a hotel at £4 per week each. Fortunately, the owner proved to be a sympathetic character (possibly due to the lack of other guests) and after a few drinks, laced with Dennis's persuasive manner, gave the jubilant threesome rooms at the vastly reduced sum of £2 *The Millionairess,* the latest comedy by George Bernard Shaw, was billed as the play that had previously brought the London press to the seaside as well as the author himself. A dog-eared press cutting explains why the great man chose Forsyth to launch his new work:-

> 'Matthew Forsyth has already been associated with Mr. Shaw by over 600 performances of *St. Joan* at the new Regent Lyceum and Her Majesty's Theatres, London. The production was also at the Champs Elysees Theatre, Paris and in Cairo and Jerusalem. Mr. Forsyth has produced many other Shaw plays including *Back to Methuselah* and *Captain Brassbounds Conversion* etc.'

Matthew must have rated highly in Shaw's esteem. Surely it was an honour for the world's most eminent author to entrust the first performance of his latest play to a repertory company. Nevertheless, even the unorthodox Mr. Shaw sometimes received double sided revues.

> 'Although *The Millionairess* is rich in dialogue, many people may now be inclined to dismiss this latest piece as a mediocre product of a brain degenerated genius. That's as maybe, but Shaw at his worst is better than the majority of dramatic authors at their best! ... topical and witty Shaw's play might be, but methinks he has swallowed a sprat and missed a mackerel.'

"Dennis and I threw a large party after *The Millionairess* to celebrate a really successful week. Playing to full houses each night doubtless gave our ego a terrific boost and we obviously felt flush in every sense of the word. We held the party at the hotel and I think my sister, Noreen, and the entire Morey family came to it."

Back to the Palace Theatre at Westcliff for an Edgar Wallace thriller, *The Case of the Frightened Lady* before moving on to the Garrick Theatre at Southport for a detective comedy, *Busman's Honeymoon.* Desmond had now been under the auspices of Matthew Forsyth for a month and was learning fast.

As the Welsh gardener, Frank Crutchley, in *Busman's Honeymoon,* his suitably suggestive lines - something to do with taking Miss Twitterton's silver tea pot up to her bedroom - brought lengthy laughter from the audience on the first night. Much to Desmond's delight, good notices followed. Yet for some baffling reason, he found on the two subsequent performances the same lines simply produced a polite titter.

"What a bloody awful audience," complained Desmond. "It's not them, it's you. You're at fault," replied Matthew bluntly. "That first night and those notices have ruined your act. Now you think you're so damned clever, you overplay the part expecting hilarious laughter each time you open your mouth and instead end up losing the audience. Be natural!"

A salutary lesson, noted, but obviously forgotten when, many years later, Desmond again referred to yet another audience as 'bloody awful'. This time, producer Wally Douglas corrected him. "It's always the actor who is wrong. Never, never the audience. If they don't get the first laugh you must double your efforts to re-capture their attention."

Another slight problem was Desmond's inability to concentrate, particularly if the part was small. His mind, forever active, roamed elsewhere and when his cue arrived, so did a mental block that called for a prompt. It would prove to be a recurring predicament throughout his acting career.

After Southport came a ten week run staging a similar number of plays at the Grand Opera House in Scarborough. The season required maximum input from every member of the company. Time came in short supply and most had to cope with a dual role. Old theatre programmes are indicative when listing the cast. In the small print below, one discovers the same names are responsible for back stage jobs like painter, assistant stage manager, stage manager, master carpenter, scenery designer and so on. Even Matthew Forsyth had to double up as actor/producer. With this type of all round experience, one can understand why it was felt the future of the English stage lay in repertory.

After two weeks in July at the Shanklin Theatre, the Forsyth players took a break for the whole of August. To take time off at the height of the season seems odd, but going on the assumption that Matthew had been unable to reserve a suitably up-market theatre, a break would be preferable to appearing in a down-market venue.

Desmond was delighted to have a holiday and went home to Ogmore-by-Sea, where Nanny clucked over his lean appearance. August passed in a pleasant haze of idleness with a visit to a Shakespeare Festival, held at Felton Rectory, near Hereford, leaving a life-long impression. In conjunction with a garden party, this yearly event was organised by the local vicar who cajoled his parishioners into taking part in a Shakespeare play every summer. The good Reverend himself would then (if he could) cast each volunteer in a role that bore a marked similarity to their own profession. So the fishmonger, still stinking of fish, would appear on stage as a fishmonger; or the gravedigger, sweaty from his exertions in the churchyard, merely had to hop over the dividing wall, spade still in hand to make his debut in the vicar's garden.

A ditty on the back page of the programme apologizes for any criticism of this refreshing adaptation:-

Hamlet at Felton
We may not be so slick
As Stratford or The Vic,
And some may think us rash
To tackle such as this.
But dear Madam, Sir or Miss
We hope you won't just say
That Felton's made a fearful hash
Of Shakespeare's greatest play.

In September 1937, the Forsyth Players re-assembled for *Bats in the Belfry* at the De La Warr Pavilion in Bexhill, East Sussex. The press suggested the residents of Bexhill met their return with a measure of relief as their summer entertainment had contained naught, but scantily clad, rather tired, overweight ladies trying to imitate a chorus line:- 'A sagging tits and bums show' was just one uncomplimentary remark.

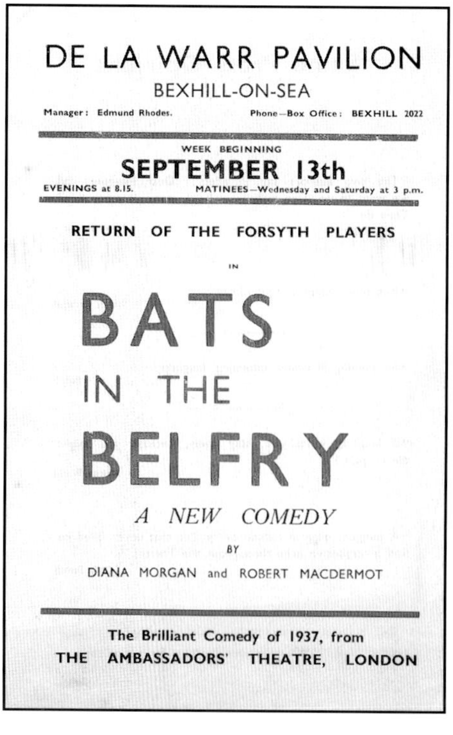
DE LA WARR PAVILION
BEXHILL-ON-SEA
Manager: Edmund Rhodes. Phone—Box Office: BEXHILL 2022
WEEK BEGINNING
SEPTEMBER 13th
EVENINGS at 8.15. MATINEES—Wednesday and Saturday at 3 p.m.
RETURN OF THE FORSYTH PLAYERS
IN
BATS
IN THE
BELFRY
A NEW COMEDY
BY
DIANA MORGAN and ROBERT MACDERMOT
The Brilliant Comedy of 1937, from
THE AMBASSADORS' THEATRE, LONDON

"BATS IN THE BELFRY"
BY
DIANA MORGAN and ROBERT MACDERMOT
Week commencing
SEPTEMBER 13th
CAST INCLUDES—
Jane Bacon
Monica Stutfield
Joy Rennie
Jane Baird
Helen Lowry
Hugh Casson
Ivan Vander
Anthony Parker
Desmond Llewelyn
Derek Tansley
Bush Bailey
Owen Jones
Gordon Brown
Play Produced by MATTHEW FORSYTH

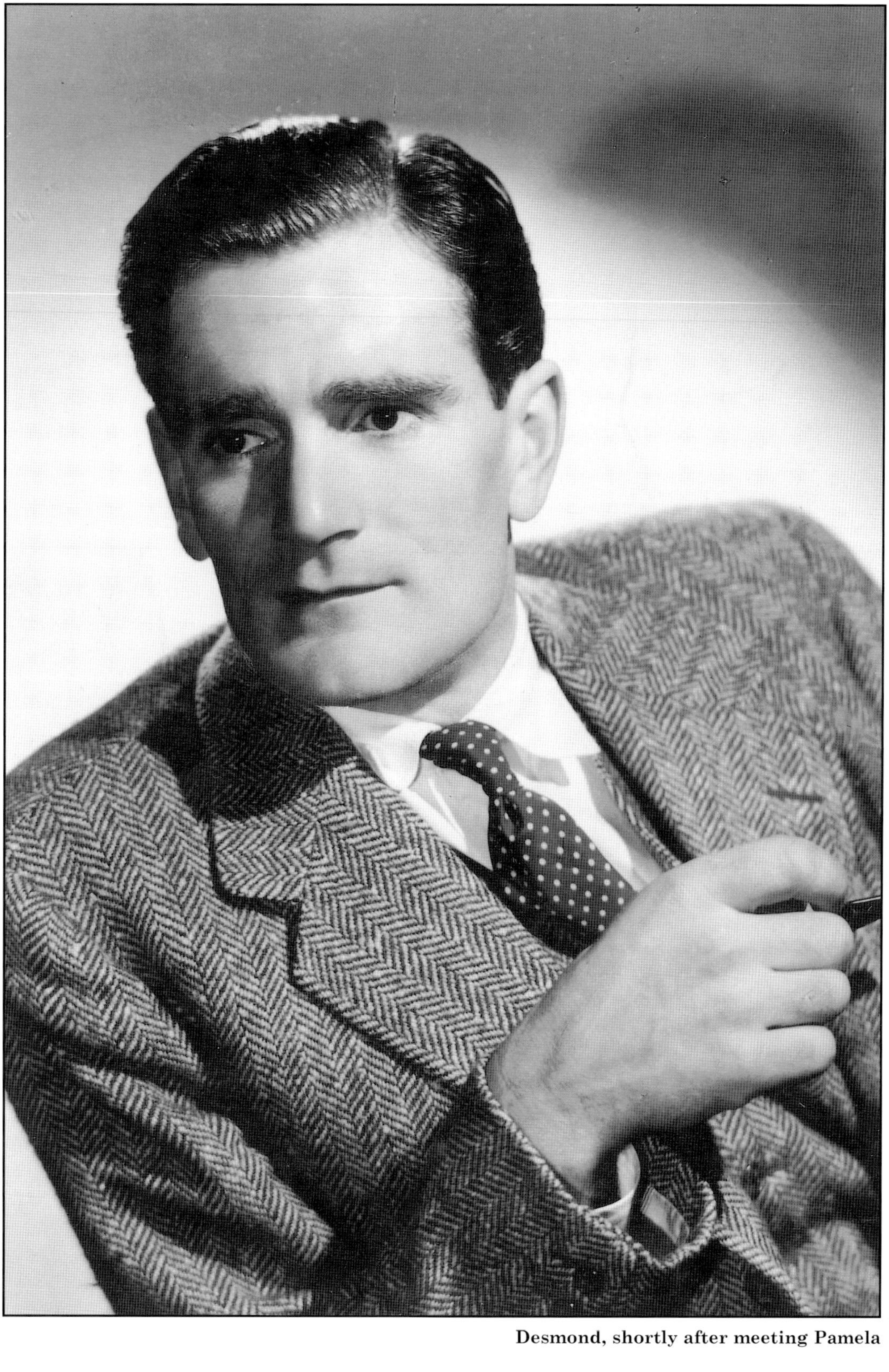

Desmond, shortly after meeting Pamela

Desmond and fellow actor, Ivan Vander, rented a cottage for the three months duration and bought an old Morris for £15. Ivan was a meticulous little man and Desmond's untidy habits drove him to distraction. "I never did a stroke of housework. Instead, I used to ask Nanny to visit and she restored order by having a jolly good tidy up."

For this autumn season of plays at the De La Warr Pavilion, Matthew found it essential to engage extra cast. Amongst them were the Pantlin twins, Diana and Phyllida, both of whom vied for Desmond's affections - he insists he did not respond to either. However, when he and Ivan held a party, Diana and Phyllida were invited. "Fortunately, they lived at Battle about ten miles distant and as neither drove they couldn't get to the party. Unfortunately, their elder sister, Pamela, stepped in and offered to act as chauffeur." Desmond met her as she dropped the twins outside and after chatting, insisted she too must stay for the evening.

The impulsive invitation issued after a few minutes conversation resulted from Desmond's attraction to her, yet he can recall his desire to impress was hampered by a sudden ineptness and garbled conversation. Pamela, unaware of his confusion, smiled, accepted his invitation and followed the twins inside, giving no further thought to the over-talkative man she'd met at the door.

Pamela Pantlin was tall, dark haired and a year or two older than her sisters. Her nose, maybe a shade too large, was redeemed by enormously expressive eyes that resisted inquisition yet portrayed a dry humour and quiet authority, giving the impression of overall beauty. School years were spent at Roedean where her intellectual abilities and organising skills made her one of the star pupils. Partially due to illness, she chose not to continue her studies by going to university and instead joined the 'Women's League of Health and Beauty'. She went on to become one of the leading lights for the southern region, where her slender figure and impeccably groomed appearance must have been the envy of many.

Her parents, Charles and Molly, lived in rather a splendid Tudor house in Battle, and as both were wealthy in their own right, their daughters were ensured of a yearly income, plus a dowry on marriage. Pamela's father, a likeable self made man whose money came from astute business transactions, also had a reputation as a lover of the ladies. Although he managed to conduct most of his affairs with discretion, the odd one or two caused tongues to wag and for a little while earned him family disapproval.

Pamela's mother, to whom she was very close, came from a long line of wealthy Sussex landowners. She was an independent lady with strong beliefs and was heavily involved in women's emancipation. Her marriage to Charles and his unfaithfulness caused, at times, deep unhappiness, but they remained together, if not in harmony, on and off throughout the years.

Meanwhile, the party was noisy and Desmond, at Pamela's elbow, pressed her to dine with him in the near future. She agreed, uncertain what to expect. She soon found out, when one week later, they arrived at Bertorellis, an overcrowded restaurant in Soho and without consulting her, he ordered one Spaghetti Bolognese and two plates! With rolls and butter the bill came to 1/6d (12p). Neither was she impressed when, anxious to demonstrate his skills at driving, he motored at high speed down a lonely stretch of road, steering with his feet and sitting on the roof of the car!

Against all odds, the romance blossomed, but as Desmond procrastinated, it was Pamela who eventually proposed to her unsuitable lover. He protested saying, "I'd love to, but I'm broke." She replied, "If you want to marry me, bugger the money." They were married within a year of meeting on 16th May 1938. He was 23, she 25. Their wedding took place at the Holy Trinity, Kensington Gore, with a reception for

Pamela on her wedding day in May 1938

about one hundred and fifty guests at The Basil Street Hotel in Knightsbridge. The groom described the days events as being similar to acting the leading role in a play. “Thoroughly enjoyable, really, except when I couldn’t get the ring on her finger. My fault, I’d bought the wrong size.” The couple spent their honeymoon exploring France and Italy taking turns at the wheel of a new MG sports car, a present from the bride’s father. Unfortunately, on the way home, another car cannoned into them from a side turning whilst Desmond was driving. “I slammed on the brakes, but nothing happened. I suppose it did bend the thing a bit, but we were OK.” Later it was proven the brakes had failed.

Desmond’s meeting and marriage to Pamela obviously took precedence above everything else, except, of course, acting. But it’s interesting to note the scrapbook, hitherto filled with photos, press cuttings, programmes and a general mish-mash of his theatrical memorabilia to date, remains from May 1938, blank.

- 4 -

FRAGMENTS FROM A P.O.W.

Warburg, 1941

"I always had a nickname. At prep school it was 'Stickjaw'.At Radley it was 'Loopy' and in the POW camps they called me 'Ham'."

- 4 -
FRAGMENTS FROM A POW

"I hope your daughter will be happy now she's wed to her penniless actor," commented Pamela's uncle tactlessly. Charles Pantlin, who had a genuine affection for Desmond, sprang to his defence. "If my daughter's happy, that's good enough for me." He failed to add that his new son-in-law shared a passion for rugger which equalled his own.

Meanwhile, in the South of France, Pamela and Desmond basked in the sun and enjoyed the trivial discoveries of a new marriage that had welded together two people of opposite extremes. The contrast in Desmond's outward and easy character to Pamela's very private temperament was noticeable in his gregarious chatter, to which she'd quietly respond with a few well chosen words. By comparison to his disorderly and chaotic approach to life, she was orderly and meticulous: later there would be his love of James Bond to her dislike of anything remotely connected with 007. Yet, in spite of the differences and often distances, each remained loyal as Pamela's less obvious persona dominated the Llewelyn household and efficiently negotiated the sometimes choppy passage. The situation was not so dissimilar to that of Ivor and Mia twenty-five years earlier.

Throughout the summer of 1938, Desmond resumed his provincial travels with Matthew Forsyth. In the October, Matthew opened for a three week run at the Peoples Palace, Mile End Road presenting *R.U.R.*; the cast included Ian Carmichael as a robot. Feeling confident of being in London for a while, Pamela and Desmond rented a flat in Doughty Street. Yet by Christmas (which was spent with his in-laws at Battle), Desmond had terminated his contract with Matthew. Again, the need to explore new pastures had crept in, or perhaps Pamela had been the instigator saying, "you can do better than that." Whatever, the time had come to put out feelers elsewhere.

In January 1939, Desmond made his first television appearance in an historical one-act play concerning Bonnie Prince Charlie. Although friends and relatives were duly informed of his forthcoming TV debut, few actually watched the play. Televisions, in those days, were scarce and most had to gather round one tiny screen centred in a cumbersome box-like object in the village hall, or better still, the local pub.

In early spring of the same year, Desmond appeared with the Principality Players and toured Wales in *Land of My Fathers* by Jack Jones. It was the first tour and presentation by an entirely Welsh company, of Welsh life, played in English. "I loved every minute of it." Pamela, however, was not quite so keen as she remained at Ogmore-by-Sea having only Mia and Nanny for company.

When the tour finished, Desmond and RADA friend, Dennis Shand established their own repertory company in Abergavenny with an input of £25 each, little knowing they were following hot on the heels of a blacklisted repertory. Small wonder that their first production, ironically called *I've Been Here Before* met with little response. However, the bonhomie and enthusiasm proved short lived and the partnership foundered when it incurred differences of opinion over casting. After four weeks, Desmond withdrew his £25 and, carefully extricating himself from any further ties, parted amicably from Dennis to look for work elsewhere.

Fortuitously, the wedding of Pamela's younger sister, Diana, to Jack Irving brought Desmond in contact with the producer of the Oxford Repertory Company, Stanford Holme - an eccentric little man with a partiality for the pretty actresses that fell under his jurisdiction. His beautiful wife bore his liaisons (including a lengthy affair with cookery writer-to-be, Elizabeth David) with enormous patience.

Stanford engaged Desmond at £5 a week and he appeared in about half a dozen productions before the theatre closed for August, Oxford's quietest month. It provided a welcome break in Stanford's exhaustive routine of twice nightly performances, six days a week:- 10.00 am: rehearsal. 2.00 pm: free time. 4.15 pm: return to theatre. 5.00 pm: first performance. 8.00 pm: second performance. 11.00 pm: supper and then afterwards the new play must be learned for the next week. Both sleep and sex were in short supply as Pamela had to sit and listen to Desmond's lines!

Meanwhile, the ambitious owner of the same repertory company, Eric Dance, had high hopes of seeing a cherished venture come to fruition at his playhouse in Oxford, where he planned to hold the European and British premieres of new plays, all staged by top London producers. The grand re-opening, scheduled for September, never materialized. Instead, Chamberlain broadcast to the nation that Britain was now at war with Germany. The country needed all its able-bodied young men to fight yet, when Desmond offered his services, he was told 'wait until you're called up'.

By chance, Pamela saw a piece in the newspaper suggesting that anybody who had been in the Officers Training Corps (at school) and achieved a Cert A, should apply immediately for a Commission in the Army. Desmond lost no time in making contact and within a few days had joined The Artist Rifles, a Territorial Army Unit. "Can I return to the theatre?" he questioned. "Of course not," came back the sobering reply from a military figure, "you're in the Army now." And after being informed they 'hadn't got a clue what happened next', Desmond found himself at Sandhurst for a ten week training by the end of September.

A handful of disjointed recollections give a brief insight into the period when Desmond was treated as one of the gentlemen cadets; memories of a nice batman who cleaned the bathroom; yawningly dull lectures pitted against the comparably chilling task of learning how to use weapons to kill; wearing a pork pie hat with full battle dress as his own didn't fit, he thinks may have demonstrated his rebellious streak against army routine - so too was his written description of a body locking device which he referred to as a 'Maiden's Delight'. "It all seemed so phoney to me. The country was at war and there we were learning about things like bugle calls from instructors who, if they'd been on the stage, would have been told they were over acting." Then it was back to Marley House for Christmas with Pamela, where the weather was so bitter that particles of ice froze the car to the driveway.

In January 1940, Desmond received the awaited commission and after an attempt at The Welsh Guards, enlisted with The Royal Welch Fusiliers. At first, the Welsh Guards had appeared to match all his requirements, until an interview with 'a snotty English Colonel' left neither impressed with the other and the application foundered. A Scotsman suggested to Desmond trying "one of the best regiments in the country, The Royal Welch Fusiliers." He did, and three months of tough training at Brecon in South Wales followed. Occasionally, Pamela came up for the weekend, stayed in the Castle Hotel and snatched a few brief hours with her husband.

Although both accepted the uncertainties of the future, reality came as an unpleasant shock when Desmond received orders to leave forthwith and join the 1st Battalion of his regiment in France. Optimistically convinced it would only be a matter of weeks before returning, he and Pamela bade hurried farewells, little realising five long years would elapse before they would meet again.

The 1st Battalion of The Royal Welch Fusiliers formed a part of the Expeditionary Force sent to France shortly after the outbreak of war. In May, after moving into Belgium to confront the advancing German Army, the BEF were forced to withdraw and start the retreat to Dunkirk. The events that lead up to a number of the men from the 1st Battalion being captured, together with Desmond's years as a POW, may be sketchy in places and therefore subject to possible inaccuracies. But whilst the past sixty years may have obliterated one or two facts, most of the events remain undimmed.

*

Somewhere on the borders of France and Belgium. *I felt totally inadequate with scant knowledge of the army and even less of war; I was an amateur amongst regulars and a mere novice as a 2nd Lieutenant and Platoon Commander in B Company. Fortunately, one of my fellow officers happened to be Michael Edwards, and as we'd been at Radley together, he provided a helpful presence.*

With a few others, I departed for France (via Southampton and Le Havre) on the 8th April 1940 and met up with the 1st Battalion at their headquarters in Mouchin. After about four weeks we were sent to guard the aerodrome at Douai. One evening I went to see an ENSA show and went backstage to meet the cast. Suddenly, the air raid sirens went, so I stayed put, drinking with them until the 'All Clear' sounded. Having arrived extremely drunk and late back at the billet, the shortened night was curtailed even further by the noise of gunfire.

The Germans had invaded and we were ordered to go and defend the River Dyle, near Ottenburg. We left Mouchin on the 11th May and reached the River Dyle the next day to take up our defensive positions in preparation for the German Army. A and C backed by D Company were close to the River Dyle; B Company remained in reserve at Ottenburg.

I think we must have been at Ottenburg about three days when a couple of my chaps asked me if they should nip across to a nearby farm and see if they could scrounge some eggs for breakfast. Momentarily I dithered, knowing I'd be court martialed if I were caught sending soldiers to collect eggs. I turned to the sergeant for reassurance, "What do you think, sarge?" "Up to you guv" came back the non-committal reply. Weakened by the vision of fresh eggs, I gave my permission and off they scarpered only to come under sudden German fire. For one awful moment, I thought I'd sent two good men to their death just for the sake of some food. My relief was paramount when they arrived back - unscathed, with the eggs unbroken. Not long after this drama the village came under an artillery attack from the Germans and that evening they shelled us even further. At 10.00 pm on 15th May, the order came through to withdraw. It was an arduous retreat, much of it on foot as the lorries had apparently gone to the wrong brigade. On Sunday 19th May we reached Tournai where we built barricades and blew up bridges. We then retreated further and by the third week in May had reached the region of Robecq, St. Floris and St. Venant, west of Lille, northwest of Bethune and close to the Belgian border. It was a beautiful spring day and somehow the sun managed to make the flat uninteresting landscape (apart from an isolated hillock) look inviting. I remember seeing a tiny church and thinking, war and religion make disturbing companions. Nothing made sense any more.

On the 25th May, instructions came through to re-take Robecq. B Company then advanced across open ground towards the village. My platoon had taken up a position in a barn, with a couple of men in the rear garden. One of them began firing at the Germans. I can see him now, tin hat on one side, cigarette in his mouth, chalking up the hits. Then, without warning, a German tank appeared in front of the barn. Misguidedly and against the advice of the sergeant, I fired the anti-tank rifle which was accompanied by a flash and immediately gave our position away. We all left pretty damn quickly by a rear entrance and continued to Robecq under the cover of nightfall.

The crossing of the Bassee Canal presented the next obstacle as several men couldn't swim. One who could, swam to a wreck in mid stream, fixed a wire hawser securely to it and then continued to the far side, thus straddling the canal. Hanging on to the wire, we managed to cross safely, but got soaking wet, so made our way towards a cottage - possibly the lock keepers - to dry off. The cottage was empty, but we searched it hoping to find food. There was none. I climbed the stairs to the attic bedroom to make a preliminary survey of the area through my father-in-law's inadequate opera glasses.

Simultaneously, and to my horror, a tank fired a shower of tracer bullets into the garden. When they stopped, a loud German voice shattered the silence. "You are surrounded. Come out with your hands up. For you the war is over."

*

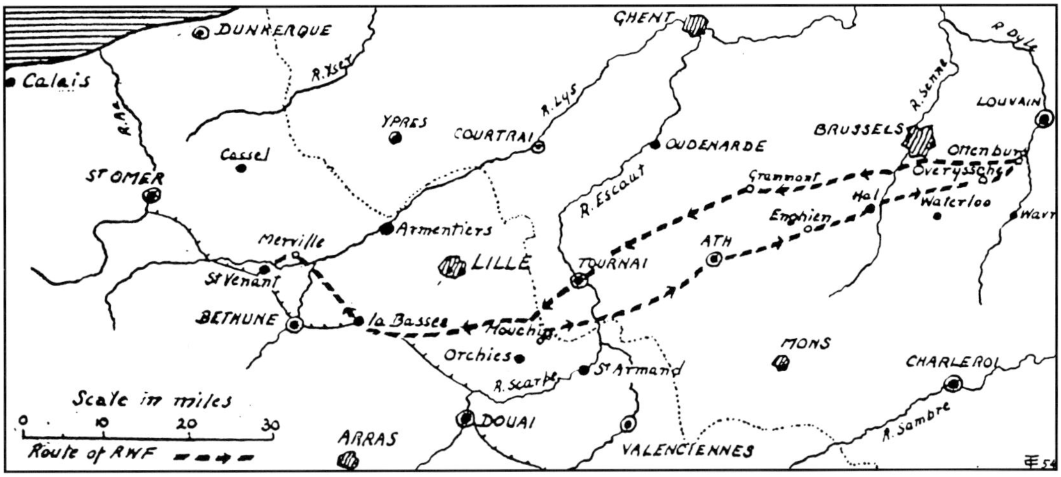

The route taken by The Royal Welch Fusiliers, May 1940

These following statistics on this situation only emerged after the war:-

'In the fighting that took place in the St. Floris, St. Venant and Robecq area between 24th and 27th May 1940, ninety-seven members of the 1st Battalion were killed in action and many more taken prisoner. Jimmy Johnson, the wounded commanding officer, successfully escaped from a prison hospital shortly after capture and became the only officer in the regiment to reach England and was later awarded the MC.'

*

Desmond was captured on the 26th May 1940 and, with his men, taken to a nearby village, where they were separated. He never saw them again. Instead, he briefly joined the Commanding Officer of B Company, Jimmy Johnson, who'd been shot through the throat. In response to the following interrogation of:- 'number, division, regiment, brigade?', Desmond pleaded ignorance and to the irritated German explained, "I'm not an officer, but an actor." Disbelievingly, the German continued his questioning, "Oh, yes, and why should an actor be in a battalion of regulars? Your men have delayed us. We need to know what we're up against. And tell me, where did you last act?" When Desmond mentioned Oxford, the interrogator showed a sudden interest, he knew Oxford well and his manner changed to the extent of sending his prisoner to the kitchens to have some chips. After a night in a prison base, Desmond, together with his captive fellow officers, were taken in cattle trucks, first to Saltzburg, then on by lorries to Laufen, a prison camp about 20 km north west of Saltzburg.

*

Laufen. *Ironically, after several days of travelling, sandwiched together more or less upright, unable to move, our main concern was constipation. However, the camp doctor assured us it was nothing to worry about. Perhaps he assumed the emotions following capture would be far more troublesome. I personally, had no feelings of degradation. After all, with hindsight, if it hadn't been for those early POWs, there would never have* been Dunkirk...! Under the pretext of hygiene, the Germans shaved our heads on arrival at Laufen; in reality it was simply to make us feel more demoralised. Conditions were pretty appalling. In our room alone there were 116 prisoners sleeping in three tier beds. This was our Mecca, we lived, ate and slept here. With only a few books and some Polish cigarettes to help pass the monotonous hours, all shreds of dignity inevitably disappeared.

By far the worst thing was being kept on starvation rations: a few slices of blackish bread, a bowl of watery soup, three potatoes and a fragment of cheese each day. I'd never realised that hunger could cause such pain. One became so weak that even walking up stairs grew to be an effort and sometimes such exertion caused blacking out.

We thought and talked food; where you could buy the best fish and chips; choosing the first meal when we got home. We could send three letters and two postcards a month (all censored, of course). I remember writing to Pamela a few weeks after capture and asking for some chocolate biscuits or indeed any non-perishable food she could muster. This had to be written in the guise of enquiring about the dog's diet. To indicate we were starving was forbidden. No such luck; six months elapsed before a food parcel of any description was allowed to be distributed.

Hunger made those initial months of imprisonment hazy and obscure. Probably things started to improve when the first Red Cross food parcels arrived and we regained some strength and equilibrium. The parcels were always shared, apportioning butter, condensed milk, spam, chocolate and porridge amongst each group. If someone could cook, he'd make up an ingenious recipe from the contents.

Prison camps varied enormously and most POWs learnt to make full use of any space available to them. For example, if the grounds were fairly extensive (and the Germans allowed it) we'd construct a football pitch, a cricket pitch or a tennis court; competitive sports acted as a balm to utter boredom. At Laufen, the grounds were minimal, but the buildings were large and rambling. Once it had been an archbishop's stately palace; now the rooms and passages were neglected and damp. But there was sufficient space in an adjacent hall to have a theatre with an orchestra (the Germans supplied the instruments). We also had a library and a school room, where one could study almost any subject from tailoring to languages or accountancy. In fact, one officer studied and passed all his exams to become a barrister. Many of the POWs were highly qualified and taught their chosen subject to anyone interested. Education offered another raison d'etre and, my goodness, we needed it.

As soon as I was fit enough, I joined forces with Bobby Loder (a regular in the Royal Sussex Regiment) to put on Escape and a review that included a sketch called Caratacus. The Germans seemed quite interested in our plays and helped by lending civilian clothes, make-up and other bits and pieces as props.

Curious as it may seem today, escaping was considered to be an officer's duty and there was no shortage of attempts at Laufen; sometimes we'd be asked to assist. More often than not this took the form of discretely distributing earth from the tunnel currently being excavated. Getting rid of earth at Laufen proved inordinately difficult. There were no flower beds or hidden corners and an increasing mound would be noticed by the guards. Instead, in the pocket of our trousers or greatcoat (depending on the weather), we'd have a small bag filled with soil. Surreptitiously, we'd drizzle the stuff from our pockets when marching around the perimeter of the walking area; each man ensuring he trod the earth scattered by the person in front, firmly into the ground.

We had access to German newspapers, but our radio provided the only real link with the news from home. God knows where we got the thing. It was, of course, strictly 'verboten' by the Germans and had to be kept hidden in the latrines where only one man, known as the 'Head News Reader', would listen to the news. He then wrote it down, gave a copy to his 'Reps' and they in turn went round and verbally relayed it.

Christmas lunch 1940. I can't recollect what we ate - not turkey anyway, but we did *have beer and with this somebody toasted the King. "We'll have a Queen next," a voice chipped in as the toast turned into a slightly fatuous debate. "We might not, the King might have more children." There was a silence as we contemplated this remark, then someone said, "Of course he won't have more children, he's much too old!" Inevitably, the question cropped up of what would happen if we lost the war. "Don't be bloody fools, of course we'll win the war," I replied with certainty to all and sundry. At home, Pamela was asking her father the same question, "Could we lose the war?" "It's possible, but highly improbable," replied Charles.*

I remained at Laufen for about a year and during the latter part caught Chicken Pox. I was immediately put into isolation and 'rested' in the comparative luxury of a sanatorium for five weeks in a proper bed where, once on the road to recovery, one of the orderlies taught us a German dance - the Shoeplatter.

*

Did the majority of POWs contemplate escape? Probably, and most of the plans would be hatched, discussed and dismissed as impossible. The rest, although rarely successful, were put into operation. This in itself was hardly a straightforward process.

First, the plan had to be organised in detail from the beginning to end, with all the risks gauged and dangers assessed before being presented to an Escape Committee for approval. Escape Committees, made up from an anonymous body of POW officers, were an integral part of every prison camp. They had been established, mainly by the army, not only to ensure the viability of each scheme, but to avoid hair-brained strategies which jeopardised the genuine escapes.

The Committee also provided a 'back up' operation to any approved plan by accessing those having the necessary expertise to facilitate the escape. The tailoring 'department' made civilian clothes. The Thomas Cook 'department' offered a complete rundown on all train timetables. The forgers 'department' printed all the false identities and the map makers somehow produced copies of maps made by using gelatine as a form of carbon paper.

*

Warburg. Late 1940 or early 1941. *One easily loses track of time as the only margins are night and day. We came here from Laufen, shoved and herded in cattle trucks. On first sight, Warburg gave the impression of being in the middle of a plain and depressingly large with masses of blackened army huts enclosed by walls of barbed wire and German guards. The entire place must have held about three thousand men, a mixed bunch from the Army, Navy and Air Force.*

The huts contained several rooms sleeping about eight. Apart from myself and John Peyton (we shared at Laufen), we had Andrew Craig Harvey, Dan Cunningham, Douglas Moyer, two others whose names remain a blank and an engineer called 'Friday' Ryan. Initially, we were a pretty despondent bunch and the foreseeable future stretched bleakly ahead. Would we ever get out of here?

I can't remember exactly when the idea of our escaping occurred, but I think John floated his thoughts as we lay on our bunks gazing vacantly at the ceiling. Of course it was hardly a new idea, most POW's spent half their waking hours planning the ultimate escape, but few came to fruition. If they did, the chaps who'd succeeded in getting out were quickly recaptured - poor sods - after all that effort.

So why should John's proposition be likely to succeed where others failed? As he outlined his plans, I think there were probably three reasons. Firstly, although the youngest, he possessed leadership qualities, secondly, those of us involved had the critical skills needed to execute his plan which thirdly, was more ambitious than anything we'd heard so far and yet sounded, in theory, simple. All we needed to do was dig a tunnel about 100 yards in length, starting underneath our elevated hut and surfacing at a discrete distance beyond the camp perimeter. Then, on an allotted day we'd slip out, two by two, trekking across Germany to Switzerland ... and freedom. Naive, especially with our schoolboy knowledge of languages, but it offered hope where there had been none and anticipation replaced lethargy. Long before the first clod of earth was dug in what became known as 'Peyton's Tunnel', we talked of getting home.

I believe about a dozen of us were involved in the escape operation. In practice, the detailed logistics appeared almost nightmarishly impossible. Particularly as every piece of vital equipment had to be made by hand from salvaged materials, or alternatively nicked from the German maintenance workers when a suitable distraction kept them busy elsewhere. Curiously, when every eventuality had been detailed and the Escape Committee had given its OK, the whole thing sounded surprisingly feasible. Perhaps the sheer enormity of the task never really dawned, but as the days were, in effect, ours, time was not a problem. We were only required to appear for a roll call in the morning and evening, otherwise the Germans, or Goons as we called them, didn't bother us except for their routine searches. The German Ferrets were something else and they were a damn nuisance. Their sole task was to slither underneath all the huts and examine the ground for signs of earth disturbance which they did with unbelievable thoroughness if they'd had an indication something was afoot.

German security search at Warburg

It was a memorable moment when we shifted the bed in the corner of our hut to cut a trap door in the floorboards below, A square of carpet, fixed to the underside, prevented echoing and a bag of carefully gathered dust filled in the cracks and concealed any incriminating evidence made by disturbance. Peyton's Tunnel had begun in earnest.

The sinking of an 8 foot shaft came next. This was positioned near to the wire at the far end of the building which, from the trap, entailed crawling about 30 foot to the 'site entrance'. At first, the digging could only be done by one or two men in the lying or crouching position, but as the tunnel itself progressed, we worked in groups of four with the day sometimes divided into two shifts. Our tools for digging were a couple of household shovels, temporarily 'borrowed' from the hut's coke burning stove, plus pieces of scrap metal fashioned into picks by putting them in the red hot embers. The earth, excavated from the tunnel, had to be distributed unnoticed in the grounds which, unlike at Laufen, was fairly easy. Some we dug into flower beds and the rest found its way into the roof space as the Germans never thought to look up there.

The shaft, about 3 foot by 3 foot and 8 foot in depth, had a trap door roughly 18 inches from the top, covered by bags of soil. This had to be replaced by one of the 'lookouts' every time the 'shift' went underground. The sides were lined at intervals with slats of wood taken from our bed bases and a goodly portion of the tunnel arched and therefore self-supporting. Initially, we used far too much wood, hence the necessity to arch and by the time the project neared completion, we were sleeping on about four slats.

At the base of the shaft, a large chamber, approximately 6 foot by 6 foot had to be formed for storage. This was christened 'Victoria' and the three subsequent, and slightly smaller chambers, 'Piccadilly', 'Charing Cross' and 'Canon Street'. The distance between each 'station' was roughly 20 yards. A sledge, again made from bed boards and hauled along on ropes, transported the earth in bags back to the guy at the bottom of the shaft who was always known as 'Arse End Charlie'.

John put me in charge of the tunnel's air supply and hundreds of butter tins rescued from Canadian Red Cross parcels formed the pipeline. These, fitted together, were sunk near the shaft into the tunnel and then buried in earth along the floor. Wholesome air then had to pumped through the line from chamber to chamber by means of bellows. We constructed three of these 'Heath Robinson' contraptions; pieces of wood and material nailed, glued, stitched and bullied into working order. For the fourth, somebody converted a gramophone. This ensured clean, fresh air as we dug. However, the system was not exactly foolproof and broke down fairly frequently, which was a ghastly feeling: the throat would tighten, eyes pop and the temperature would rise until emergency repairs restored it. Suddenly, I understood how a fish suffers and have been against fishing as a sport ever since.

The tunnel illuminations were another priority and although electrics didn't come into my area, I remember bits of wire and tar substituting flex and having to pinch light bulbs from the hut. More importantly, the illuminations acted as an early warning system. One click from the look-outs meant the Ferrets were on the prowl: two clicks and they were in the vicinity - stop working: three clicks and the lights went off - danger imminent.

Even in the 'danger imminent' situation I felt oddly secure tucked down there amongst the worms and came to the conclusion I was more of a collier's son than previously realised. Digging through the depths of the earth held no horrors and I used to hum Beethoven's Violin Concerto whilst lying on my side wielding a shovel.

From memory, the tunnel took about six months to complete and as the end came in sight we viewed it with mixed emotions. The tunnel had been our life line, a safety net holding a secret camaraderie between us. Shortly we'd escape and then ... who knows, it would probably be every man for himself. As the day drew close, we prepared to collect our rations together with some chocolate, maps, a small amount of cash and a compass; by today's standards, paltry equipment for escaping, but all that could be managed under the circumstances. Now we required a pitch black night without a trace of moonlight and a lot of luck.

I think it was a Thursday when I and two others went down into the tunnel to make some final preparations before the exodus. Suddenly, the lights flicked off; once, twice, three times. We waited, silent and rigid. I was by the shaft when I heard the thump of bayonets on the earth above, a clicking noise, then a crash. The Ferrets had struck the air line. All our work ...

Perhaps we never really expected to escape from Warburg, although as 'Friday' said afterwards, "it would have been nice to get out if only to see the countryside!" Instead we were rounded up, photographed and after a couple of days, accompanied by guards, sent to Paderborne (a cooler or 'khuler') for ten days. I had my own cell which was absolute bliss after sharing with so many.

With hindsight we were lucky and got off fairly lightly; Peyton's tunnel, however, had a more unfortunate end. To ensure it could never be used again, the Germans de-gorged tons of raw sewage from their culture wagon down the shaft before finally sealing up one of the longest escape routes to the outside world.

Thereafter, the tunnel became part of Warburg's history as one of the four (out of seventy-four dug in that one year) to surface on the right side of the wire.

The whole episode cured me of ever attempting to break out again. Resigned to a POW existence for as long as it took to win the war, I left escaping to others, but became actively involved in helping them try and get out. I endeavoured to learn Welsh, thinking for some reason a knowledge of the language might be a useful adjunct for the Escape Committee and wrote a coded postcard in Welsh to my father-in-law appealing for secret maps and books. Obviously misunderstood, back came the bald reply via the committee. 'Contact Llewelyn. He wishes to escape!!' Some years later when I questioned Pamela about this incident, she told me she'd asked the lay preacher, Mr. Thomas, to translate the message and he'd implied I was requesting contraband equipment which wasn't allowed!

That famous, legless pilot, Douglas Bader, had a room in our hut and I got to know him when I carted a gramophone around to play records to the POWs. We actually got on quite well. On one occasion, when the guards had to be distracted because another escape was in operation, we took his legs in ritual horseplay tossing them around the parade ground like tin sticks. His pre-planned anger kept the guards suitably amused.

*

Light-hearted letters, mostly from Pamela, helped boost morale and kept Desmond abreast of family news. However, occasionally they held sad tidings and when he read of Mia's death in 1942, the extraordinary sense of loss seemed out of proportion for the mother he'd never really known or been close to; possibly his isolation and ignorance of her illness added a kind of sub-conscious guilt feeling.

If Desmond had analysed the situation, he'd have realised Mia, on learning she had cancer, coped as she always had done, by subjugating her private emotions, telling no one and putting on a 'normal' face to the outside world. Apart from her sister, only Nanny knew of her illness and was with her when she died at a nursing home in Ross-on-Wye. 'Mercifully,' said Pamela's letter, 'the end had been brief.'

Less than a year earlier, Mia had been outwardly healthy and attended Noreen's wedding to Desmond's erstwhile friend, Peter Morey. It was a marriage engineered by Peter's scheming old mother and not destined to last. A daughter, Mia, after her grandmother, was born in 1942. The long on-off separations resulting from Peter's naval career, his philandering and Noreen's apparent sexual frigidity, led to an inevitable breakdown and as the war finished, so did their marriage; little Mia remaining with her mother. Peter eventually re-married and Noreen went into business with a friend and established a small school.

At home, Pamela added her contribution to war efforts. In the early days, she and her mother, with a band of volunteers, opened a much needed canteen in Battle for the Canadian troops billeted in the area. Anxious to harness her considerable capabilities to the full, Pamela joined the ATS in 1941 with the former top model, Mary Pitman, a friend from Battle. After assessment she was posted to an Officers' Training Unit in Edinburgh. Having got her commission, she was then sent to a mixed unit at Blackdown. Here, the regimental routine suited Pamela's efficient personality and enabled her to sail effortlessly up the ranks to become a Major in 1942. For the rest of the war, she stayed attached to the Royal Holloway College as an instructor.

Pamela, 1942

Douglas Bader

Bobby Loder

Frank Slater (artist)

Dan Cunningham

Desmond 'Ham' Llewelyn

Michael Goodliffe

Brian McIrvine

Wally Finlayson

Caricatures drawn whilst in prison, of Desmond and his companions, including the artist, Frank Slater

*

Eichstatt. *What a relief to leave the dreariness of Warburg. A cheer went up when the Goons announced we'd be moving. They packed the RAF off to a Luftwaffe camp and I believe those who had VIP connections were sent either to Colditz or Spangenberg. The rest of us came to Eichstatt in Bavaria. We travelled here by train and even though heavily accompanied by German soldiers, the journey bore the essence of a holiday atmosphere.*

It must have taken about twenty-four hours and on arrival at Eichstatt, we alighted from the train to be marched hurriedly to the camp; a disused barracks about ten minutes from the town centre. The buildings were on two levels. I was in the upper section in a room that held ten. It was good to be back with an entirely army crowd and my immediate companions were an up market lot who referred to The Savoy as their local pub.

It felt almost like an oversized boarding house, until we met our objectionable little Kommandant, by the name of Blattenbaur. He lost no time in throwing his weight around and within a few days ordered the officers to be manacled for an unspecified length of time from morning to evening. We gathered this instruction had come via Hitler and stemmed from a series of reprisals apparently caused by our Commando raids and the binding of their prisoners.

With a little practice we got fairly adept at slipping out of the handcuffs and leaving them dangling on one wrist, ready to clip them back at a moments notice. Although one POW, unaware of the impending visit by the Swiss Commission, was found lying on his bed smoking with the handcuffs hanging over the bed rail. The guards were obviously a bit ashamed of this order and pretended not to be aware of our Houdini talents.

At Eichstatt, I threw myself seriously into acting and reaped the benefit of working with several professionals: Brian McIrvine, Dan Cunningham, Wally Finlayson (stage name, Douglas), whose brother was a Hollywood actor, and Michael Goodliffe. I'd seen Wally, an experienced professional, on the London stage before the war and Michael, a charming man with plenty of natural ability, eventually made quite a name for himself in TV and films.

The theatre at Eichstatt was small and Wally made a superb job of producing plays under restricted conditions. His productions were: The Frightened Lady, Man of

Eichstatt. Desmond (centre stage) in *The Frightened Lady* produced by Wally Finlayson

Destiny, *the premiere of* Post Mortem *and a pantomime, but his praise was sparing and I don't think he thought much of me as an actor.*

Unforseen jaw problems occasionally interfered with rehearsing as the damn thing kept slipping out. 'Due to lack of fat in your diet,' I was told by the doctor who clicked the thing back into place. To have this done, I'd been escorted to a hospital by a guard and as we walked along the street, a Jew wearing the enforced Star of David happened to get in the way. Instantly, the guard struck him in the stomach and the man crumpled into the gutter like a fallen leaf. A cruel incident that left a poisonous taste. Later, I witnessed another disturbing scene at the hospital whose inmates, instead of being wounded, had suffered extreme frostbite on the Russian front and lay in agony waiting for limbs to be severed.

The Old Radlean Society was, in a roundabout way, responsible for my having a reasonable diet in Eichstatt (albeit lacking in fat). They used to send me a couple of hundred cigarettes each week and most of these were bartered for food with the Germans, all avid smokers of English fags.

*

The entire cast in the premiere of Post Mortem at Eichstatt

One vivid memory Desmond has of Eichstatt, is the British head of canteen blackmailing the German head of canteen into obtaining certain accessories to facilitate some POWs planning to escape as Generals. As the German in question regularly accepted coffee and cigarettes from the British he was deemed a suitable Goon to approach. In response to their request for the badges and epaulets of German Generals, he came back with the expected negative reply. But his prisoners were suitably prepared and said, "Look here, you fraternize with us, take our coffee and cigarettes. Suppose we complained, just think how seriously your superiors would take that; you'd be sent to the Eastern Front and it's very cold out there..." Within two days they had everything they needed.

Desmond remained in Eichstatt for a year, then at the end of 1943 he moved to Rotenberg. The war had begun to turn slightly in our favour and most POWs felt the end might be in sight.

*

Rotenberg. *Another train journey brought us to Jacob's Grimms, a former girl's school and really very pleasant. Regulations were a little more lenient, except here the Goons had a nasty habit of ordering everybody to appear on parade at some crazy hour during the night. To be turfed out of a warm bed into the freezing cold and then made to stand for 30 or 40 minutes is hell: you never get warm again.*

Although no actual theatre existed within the complex of Rotenberg, the dining room offered a makeshift stage. This would have to be assembled in a frantic rush after the evening meal and cleared away again when the performance ended.

I did quite a bit of producing and once inveigled two burly Scotsmen to play Noel Coward and Gertrude Lawrence in Private Lives. *The amorous honeymoon scene spoken in thick, deep Scottish accents kept the audience, and me even more so, highly amused. I subsequently worked on a couple of reviews, adapted* A Christmas Carol, *then acted in* Middle Watch *and* A Midsummer Night's Dream. *The Germans, particularly one who'd been a theatre critic in Berlin ,always watched the plays, taking photos and providing us with civilian costumes, wigs and Leichner make-up. Probably we were even better equipped than our own English stage.*

Lights had to be out by ten o'clock unless an extension had been granted due to a performance. This came to an end during 1944 when heavy bombing occurred, so we watched our only film, featuring Rita Hayworth, and listened to records instead. One of my room mates would lie on his bunk for hours playing Vera Lynn songs and smelling a bar of Lux soap. God knows what fantasies were drifting through his mind.

I can't recollect the order of events in those final weeks in 1945, but the war was definitely going badly for Germany and we were told to prepare to move on, maybe into the mountains or Bavaria; the air was thick with rumours. Uncertain where we were heading we left Rotenberg and feeling weary after days of fruitless marching, were billeted in a village hall. My feet hurt and I was buggered if I was going to walk any further. Mustering all my acting abilities, I, with about fifteen others, got the doctors to agree we could be taken on by lorry that evening; the rest must continue marching. We knew the Americans were in the vicinity and after the others had gone ahead there were bursts of gunfire and some almighty crashes as buildings caught alight, then toppled to the ground. The next thing I remember is peering through the dirty cellar windows of a hotel and saying to the chap next to me, "Who the hell do those tanks belong to? They've got a star on, surely they can't be Russian?" "Those tanks," he replied with barely concealed excitement, "are American." He was right, but as the Americans appeared to be shooting indiscriminately, we approached them hesitantly. The first question the GIs asked was, "how long have you been prisoners?" When we replied, "Five years," they said: "Don't be stupid, the war hasn't been on that long!"

At last the fighting was over; we'd been liberated by General Patton's GIs and soon we'd be reunited with our families. The Americans transported us to their Lucky Strike camp in France, where they played 'God Save The King' and wished us a pleasant stay. But we had no intention of staying and a short while later the RAF flew us back to Brize Norton, each one of us taking a turn at looking out of the cockpit window, impatient to catch our first glimpse of home. From Brize Norton we were taken to Chalfont St. Peter and as we cheered the wonderful sight of a blue-uniformed 'bobby', I happened to note the date, 8th April 1945 - exactly five years to the day since I'd left England.

- 5 -

BITS AND PIECES

"Oh, to play the man in the foreground instead of the blur in the background."

- 5 -
BITS AND PIECES

The astringent climate of post war Britain could hardly be described as lucrative for the theatrical profession. Sundry agencies and clubs, usually set up by former actors, offered assistance in finding work. A Jeffrey Robinson devoted his company entirely to ex-Army officers who, like himself, acted before the war. William Fox ran the Reunion Theatre with a bunch of willing volunteers that included Desmond. Initially, the plays William presented were under painfully basic conditions and often the participants had to wear their own clothes; costumes were a forgotten luxury. The Services Sunday Society staged one day performances, every audition being vastly overcrowded with hopeful ex-actors. Sadly, Eric Dance, the ambitious and go-ahead owner of the Oxford Playhouse, had been brutally murdered by the Japanese during the 1940's. His theatre, which could have offered so much, had been half-heartedly taken over by his Box Office lady, known only as Celia.

Having been reunited at the Savoy Hotel, Desmond and Pamela found a home after their advertisement, 'Ex POW wants somewhere to live', elicited a response from a dentist with a flat in Elizabeth Street above his dental practice. "So useful for emergencies." Battling with the vagaries of wartime pay gave Desmond a fair slice of ready cash, but not as much as he'd hoped. To his anger, he learned a large chunk of his salary had been deducted for his board and lodging as a POW. "An unforgivable piece of bureaucracy that still incenses me today." However, Pamela's private income provided a welcome mainstay, although, with hindsight, Desmond admits this possibly caused a certain complacency in his attitude. "As an actor, it's better to be hungry - you try that much harder."

In 1946, producer Robert Atkins put on *Golden Eagle,* a play about Mary Queen of Scots, at the Westminster Theatre. In his first post war job as understudy to Torin Thatcher's Bothwell, Desmond sat in the wings night after night until Torin kindly feigned illness. For just one glorious performance he played opposite the lovely Clare Luce; a telegram from Torin on the day reads:- 'From Bothwell to Bothwell. Knock 'em.'

His next appearance, in Liverpool, was in another Robert Atkins production *As You Like It,* followed by Robert's series of Shakespeare plays at the open-air theatre in Regent's Park. Robert was over sixty by now and had a formidable reputation for skilful and versatile adaptations. "He was a cantankerous old bastard, highly intelligent with a wicked choice of words - we all loved him and his outspoken comments were legendary. I'll never forget his advice about one Shakespeare scene where I had to woo a nervous and very hesitant young actress into making love. 'Well, show some excitement girl, show some excitement,'he rasped loudly. Minutes later, his voice echoed across Regent's Park once again. 'Close your legs girl, close your legs. You're anticipating the entrance by at least forty-eight hours!' We just curled up and laughed."

At Stratford, on another occasion, the time honoured routine for the resident producer to read the lesson on Shakespeare's birthday went awry. Somehow Robert was overlooked. Visibly irritated, he approached the vicar and said, for everybody within earshot to hear, "tell me old son, is there any cogent reason why I should not be allowed to read your fucking lesson?"

Shakespeare. Behind the scenes at the Open Air Theatre in Regent's Park

With the same cast, *As You Like It* was broadcast live for television from Ally Pally (Alexandra Palace). Suitably apprehensive at this new medium, the players were told, "If you dry up, keep your mouth moving; the public won't know - promise."

In the autumn of 1946, Pamela and Desmond went on holiday to the west coast of Ireland where Pamela had family connections (her great grandfather had been vicar of Westport and her mother had an ex-boyfriend still in the area). They travelled to Co. Mayo, via Liverpool and Dublin. Ireland had been badly affected by the war and in most areas spartan conditions still applied. There was virtually no petrol, no coal (turves were burnt instead), and much of the gas had been turned off. The train journey of less than two hundred miles from Dublin took ten hours. Worse still, torrential rain beset them as they stepped onto the station platform and were blown towards the Southern Hotel in Mulraney by a howling gale. A blazing peat fire, a friendly welcome, a dinner of steak and eggs washed down with red wine altered their perspective of the place. There was absolutely no sign of food rationing. "We hadn't seen steak for years. It was also a relief to find an unending supply of wine as Pamela's father had stayed the year before and reckoned he might have drunk it all."

Intermittent appearances with the Services Sunday Society in co-operation with Reunion Theatre Association at the Whitehall Theatre, preceded a part in *Warrant for your Arrest*. The play gave Desmond the part of Chief Inspector Horner and an opportunity to tour the major cities of England.

In May 1947, he was offered a 'blur in background', as non-speaking roles were called, in the film production of *Hamlet* at £10 a day - guaranteed £350. It seemed like a fortune and not one to be turned down. The film starred Laurence Olivier and a young newcomer, Jean Simmons, who played Ophelia; some thought she bore an uncanny similarity to his wife Vivien Leigh. Apart for a penchant for beautiful women, Olivier was well know for his sarcastic wit and as he watched one unknown actor jogging around the studio is reputed to have said. "Dear boy, what on earth are you doing?" "I need to be out of breath for the next scene," the novice answered. The great man paused before replying. "Dear boy, why on earth don't you try acting instead?"

The lure of Ireland, coinciding with a break in *Hamlet,* proved irresistible and Pamela and Desmond took a short holiday in Co. Mayo before he returned to Denham studios. Prior to this, negotiations concerning the sale of the freehold land forming a part of the Blaen-y-pant estate had taken up much of his spare time.

When Ivor had died in 1930, the impending bankruptcy had forced Mia to sell the main house of Blaen-y-pant outright to pay debts. The solicitor then advised her to let out the remaining two cottages, plus the estate land, on a long tenancy, so retaining the freehold and an annual income from the ground rents. This amounted to approximately £300 a year and on Mia's death it passed to her two children. They, in turn, now needed capital not income; Desmond to buy a London home and Noreen to help equip the school she ran with her friend, Mrs Hillsden.

A. Scott & Block & Webbs of Newport auctioned the Blaen-y-pant land and cottages on 2nd April 1947. The lots totalled nine and Desmond, incognito at the back of the room, listened to the fields he'd roamed across as a boy sell at £14,000 for building houses, and flats.

Within a few months the divided cash had purchased a house in Blantyre Street where Pamela fell into the role of a full-time housewife with comparative ease. She had no wish to capitalize on her obvious capabilities and find another career. Her forte, it seems, lay within the privacy of her own four walls. The longed for family had not yet materialised and for a while, Pamela concentrated on her culinary skills. Dinner guests were often glamourous: Jack Hawkins and his pretty girlfriend,

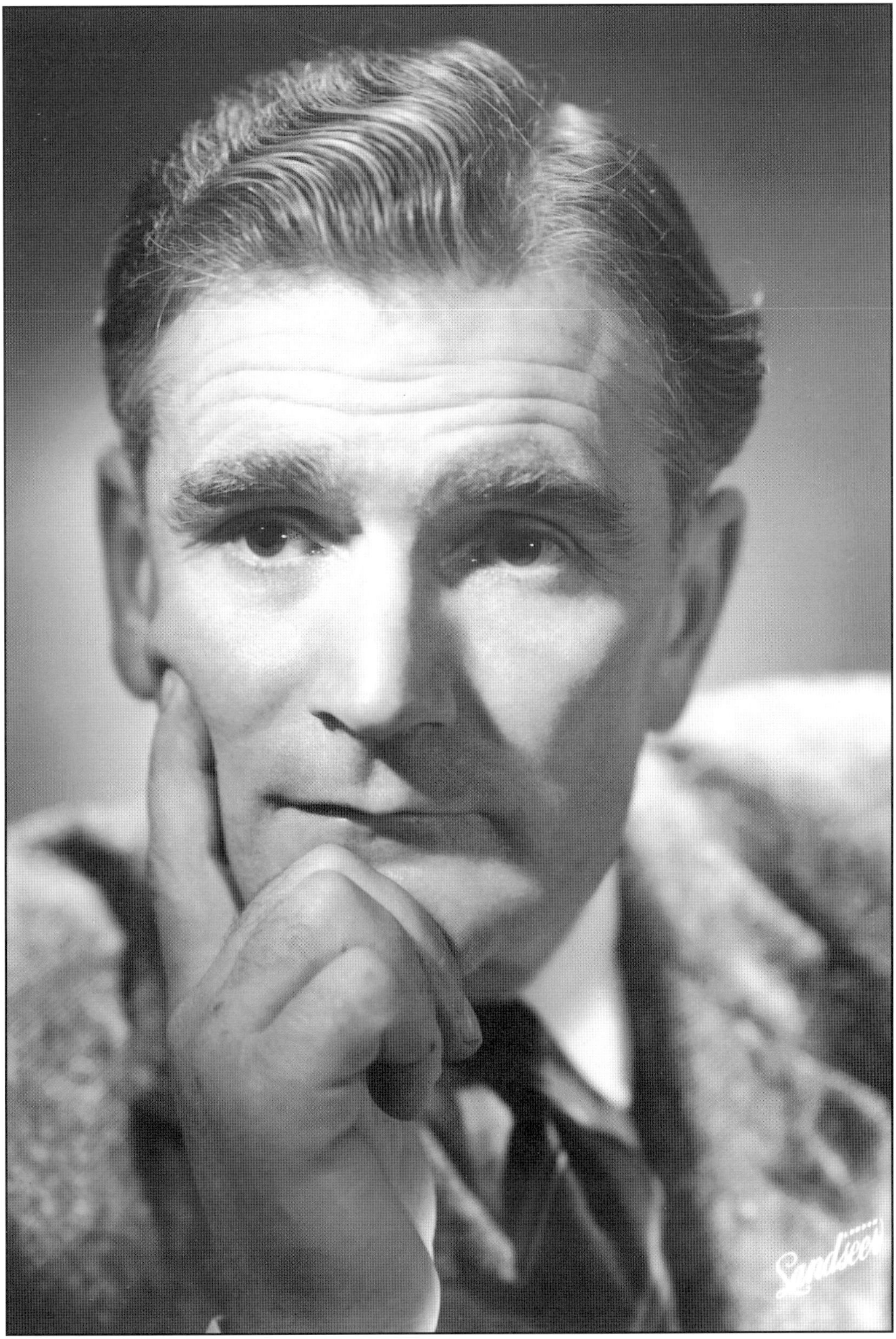

Desmond's first 'agency' photo after the War

Doreen; producer, Robert Atkins; Hugh Griffiths; Diana Morgan with her husband, Robert MacDermot.

Diana was currently appearing in *The Comedy of Good and Evil* alongside Desmond as Owain Flatfish; Hugh Griffiths had been cast in the principal role of the Vicar. "Hugh was a frightful old rogue and kicked up a helluva stink because the Vicar dies off in the second act and only his voice is heard thereafter. He wanted to remain on the stage throughout and, in the dress rehearsal, refused to continue unless his wish was granted. After a hurried meeting, he was informed neither the owner, nor author, nor the producer (a woman) wanted him in the last act. He sulkily capitulated and, with a parting jibe, said, "I do not consider Vivienne Bennett a producer."

Good Companions; The Scarlet Pimpernel; The Burning Bush; Granite; radio and more TV work back at Ally Pally filled the days. Subsequently, *The Cat and The Canary* opened to excellent reviews in Bournemouth and starred Peggy Evans. As usual, Desmond's role was frustratingly minimal, but it left him plenty of time to observe his favourite stand-up comedian, Clapham, who was amongst the company. Before going on tour, the *Canary* cast threw an eminently successful party. "After which," states Desmond with the utmost conviction, "we conceived our first child."

As yet oblivious of conception, Pamela accompanied Desmond to Edinburgh with *The Cat and The Canary.* Here, the chambermaid burst into their bedroom at an ill chosen moment shouting, "A Prince is born; we have a Prince and a future King!".

At some point during those few months of the late 40s (or maybe it was the early 50s), Desmond had a brush with God on his way to theatre in Scunthorpe. He was driving with three passengers rather too fast when he came to a sharp bend. Unable to slow down, the car continued ahead, passing under a lych gate and gently turning over, it came to rest on its roof in front of the church. Doubtless this was a fortuitous place, but as the occupants scrambled out unhurt, they came face to face with an irate verger. "Get that thing out of here, we've got a service in a minute!" The police were duly called and they peered quizzically at the damaged vehicle. "That's very odd. We've had one car over here before and another one over there, but nobody's ever survived." "That's as maybe," replied Desmond, "but I have yet to face my mother-in-law, it's her car."

Apart from a doubtful film *Adam and Evelyn* and another *The Chiltern Hundreds,* plus a few flattering television appearances, free time far outweighed any work. In search of this essential commodity, Desmond followed the common practice and did the rounds of likely pubs where film or television directors and producers were known to drink. It paid off when seated at the bar, glass in hand, the owner of a welcomed voice said, "Look I don't usually cast in a pub, but what are you doing on Thursday?"

At the beginning of the year things looked up when a screen test on the 24th/25th January 1949 secured Desmond the role of '77 Jones', a Welsh tank driver in the wartime epic *They Were Not Divided.* Shooting took several months and began in May at Denham Studios and in Germany. Fortunately, '77 Jones' arrived back from location in Hamburg in time for the birth of his first son, Ivor, on the 14th July 1949, yet typically, the only scrap of information in his diary for that memorable day is: 'On standby for filming'.

They Were Not Divided was a legendary wartime tale after Desmond's own heart. He has nothing but praise for director, Terence Young, who depicted a lifelike re-enactment of just one small part of the last war. The film is chiefly concerned with a Battalion of the Welsh Guards and covers their training from Dunkirk to D-Day and active service thereafter. Human relationships play a prominent part: the two friends who serve and die together; a few impeccably groomed women are in a constant state

On location for *They Were Not Divided.* Director, Terence Young in the foreground of bidding a tearful farewell to uniformed soldiers; shots of Montgomery and Eisenhower give an overriding presence and a certain authenticity. This, together with a bewildering cavalcade of noisy action, ensured the film contained all the ingredients for an instant success.

From a personal angle, Desmond hoped this could be his big break. As '77 Jones', he had the chance to air both a Welsh accent and his acting abilities in the largest role of his career so far. He was nevertheless annoyed when he discovered several amateurs with even better parts in the film. "One of them was the fabulously moustached Trubshawe, who played 'The Major'. He ran a pub in Rye and that's where Terence met him. I believe he got a lot of work afterwards, which was galling because I didn't."

The Premiere of *They Were Not Divided* took place at The Leicester Square Theatre in March 1950. Its pre-forecast success proved correct. The public loved it. The poignancy, the humour, the pride and even the despair touched their hearts and the cinemas were filled to capacity.

For Desmond the success of *Divided* was marred by illness when he was rushed home from an after premiere party at the Caprice, feeling "perfectly bloody". Doctors diagnosed severe jaundice and for the next two months he was unable to work. On reflection, this malaise could have been responsible for altering the expected course of events when he had to turn down a leading role at Kew Theatre. "After that, everything went eerily quiet. Even the pre-planned move into a house in Chelsea Park Gardens, which I had to negotiate in pyjamas, appeared to be undertaken in a suppressed silence."

Having been finally declared fit, Desmond took a regrettably insignificant part in *The White Eagles,* written by his friend Diana Morgan and produced by an even older friend, Wally Douglas. Again Wally reminded him that he needed to choose his parts carefully. "You're not a good enough actor to cope with anything you're unhappy in." Perhaps his words had a subconsciously damning effect, resulting in Desmond's acceptance of the 'blur in the background' roles.

In 1951 Desmond again worked with Laurence Olivier, appearing in the alternating *Caesar and Cleopatra* and *Anthony and Cleopatra.* After touring, the plays came to the St. James Street Theatre in London, a beautiful old building, now demolished.

"Apart from being a soldier in a couple of crowd scenes, I was Olivier's understudy, but I'm not sure why they chose me; I'm so bad at Shakespeare." Nevertheless, he enjoyed the production and found its long list of stars - the Oliviers, Peter Cushing, Wilfrid Hyde White, Elspeth March, Jill Bennett, Maxine Audley and Robert Helpmann - were extremely friendly. "I remember Helpmann's brother, Max, a broad Aussie, opening beer bottles with his teeth. I don't know if he could do anything else."

Although he'd met her before, it was the first time Desmond had worked with Vivien Leigh. He found her an utter delight and very helpful. However, her volatile personality masked ongoing threats of severe depression leaving Laurence Olivier in a constant state of fear lest the latter suddenly erupted with a terrifying force. Inevitably, this put an enormous strain on their relationship and even the cast noticed an increasing disharmony between them as Olivier grew more remote and Vivien touchy.

The demanding duo of plays, one concerned with the young and the other an older, Cleopatra, were both portrayed by the versatile Vivien helped by a skilled make-up artist. The production enjoyed a six month stretch in this country and, with the Oliviers, went on to have an equally successful spell in America. Although Desmond turned down the offer to go with the rest of the cast, he and Pamela were invited to a sensational last night party (thrown by Olivier Productions) on board a large boat on the Thames.

Persistent stomach cramps pre-empted another health problem. At Pamela's insistence, Desmond went to see a doctor who suggested it could be a grumbling appendix and not a duodenal ulcer as he'd feared. An operation and a few weeks convalescence by the sea in Bexhill ensured he was fit enough to look after Pamela when their second son, Justin, was born in 1952.

The pre-planned Caesarian birth was slightly earlier than expected and its unlikely cause lay with a solid downpour of rain. A couple of days before she was due to go into hospital, a heavily pregnant Pamela answered an urgent knock on the door. Her surgeon stood there clad in plus fours, a sports jacket and a cap. "Sorry to bother you," he said, "but my game of golf's been cancelled because of the bad weather. D'you mind if I do your operation instead?"

Infinitesimal parts over the next two years left Desmond frustrated and his ebullient character showed signs of strain. Pamela, whilst brusquely dismissive of the acting fraternity (even her husband) remained supportive. Sensibly, she pointed out that collectively his appearances were not insubstantial:- a play based on that popular radio programme, *The Archers* had toured the country with Desmond as Dan Archer: films such as *The Lavender Hill Mob* and *Knights of The Round Table:* TV appearances in *My Wife Jacqueline, Striker of The Yard* and then four weeks in another play called *The Crooked Finger.* "Add these," said Pamela, "to a score of tiny unmentioned appearances makes your last two years sound quite impressive."

To a certain extent, 1954 tipped the balance in another direction when Desmond appeared in the Agatha Christie thriller *The Spider's Web;* a contract that kept him in the West End theatre for nearly three years. "Towards the end, I began to feel like a civil servant wearing the same clothes and going to the same place at the same time every day."

The play with Margaret Lockwood opened first in Nottingham, then went on to Newcastle, Liverpool, Edinburgh, Coventry, Birmingham, Leeds, Oxford, Cardiff and Southsea. It was then presented in London at the Savoy Theatre. As Constable Jones, Desmond's lines were woefully inadequate. However, his silent presence was required on stage during most of the second act in the guise of a policeman taking notes. To avoid falling asleep he kept a diary, filled with doodles and some revealing one-liners. The cover is headed, 'P.C. Daffyd Bleedyn Jones Diary':-

> Rained all day - sized ceiling - lunch with Tony Blair - oiled gramophone - rehearsal 3.30 pm - left Battle 1.15 pm - England 300 to win, Australia 257, England 72 for 2 - cleaned off ceiling and gave a coat of emulsion - no play in Test - took Justin shopping - washed ceiling and filled in cracks - painted floor (a change from ceilings) - sorted out coal - painted kitchen - I HATE PLAYING POLICEMEN.

The text continues in the same idiom before ending in another flourish - I'M BORED. Fleetingly, an offer made by a local builder sounded tempting. 'You can come and work for us, mate; plenty to do 'ere.'

Written in a cramped hand on the final pages of the diary is a charming, but unfinished missive on Desmond's favourite breed of dogs, Corgis:-

> This is Troidwen and he's a Pembrokeshire Corgi. We found him in a pet shop in the North End Road. He was sitting in the window looking up at the sky. The woman said he was looking for buzzards! I called him Troidwen because he has four white feet and his name is Welsh for 'white foot'. My wife thinks it's a silly name. "After all," she said, "he's not been born in Wales, he's not going to live in Wales and he doesn't have a Welsh bark." But Troidwen he remained.

The piece goes on to tell of the idiosyncrasies of owning a Corgi puppy before petering out. Apparently, it was intended to be completed and presented to the BBC for a children's programme.

Pamela also did some writing. The spell of routine enforced by *The Spider's Web* meant she had free time every evening after the children were in bed and Desmond had left for the theatre. Her attempts at two plays were highly praised by Terence Rattigan. The first, *Comfort Me With Apples,* she wrote under the pseudonym of Mary Rivers. "There was a wonderful part for me in it, but she never bothered to complete the thing."

The second play, *Each Wind That Blows,* Pamela found more of a challenge and had no hesitation in writing under her own name. It was produced in London to favourable reviews which instigated several enquiries from interested agents. But Pamela's enthusiasm had waned and she shooed them away like flies. Her need to write had been transient; convenient, pleasant and a time filler. Now it was of no further use. She didn't need the money it could bring. She didn't want to lose her self-imposed privacy and she certainly didn't want to be beholden to the whims of public criticism. Glory of any sort was unimportant.

Although *The Spiders Web* placed obvious restrictions on Desmond accepting other work, there were a few radio broadcasts including the 'pinny and curlers' programme, *Housewives Choice.* But he longed for a change. The familiar Wally Douglas, producer of *Spiders Web* turned a deaf ear on Desmond's pleas of transferring to a better part when one of the cast vacated. "He was a so-and-so and he reiterated that I'd be better in films or TV. Pamela agreed with him. She said I had no sense of rhythm; couldn't sing or dance and found difficulty in learning lines. This, plus the fact somebody once told me, to be a successful actor you need balls that jangle like temple bells - which I hadn't - suggested I was doomed to failure."

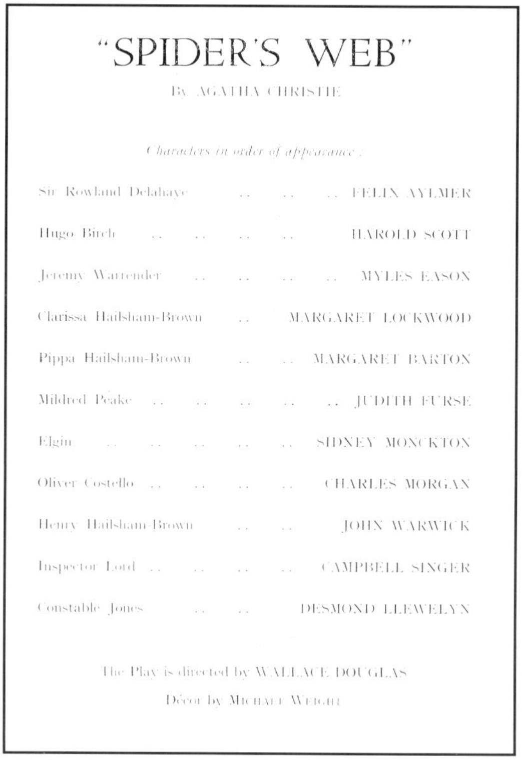

"SPIDER'S WEB"

BY AGATHA CHRISTIE

Characters in order of appearance :

Sir Rowland Delahaye	FELIX AYLMER
Hugo Birch	HAROLD SCOTT
Jeremy Warrender	MYLES EASON
Clarissa Hailsham-Brown	MARGARET LOCKWOOD
Pippa Hailsham-Brown	MARGARET BARTON
Mildred Peake	JUDITH FURSE
Elgin	SIDNEY MONCKTON
Oliver Costello	CHARLES MORGAN
Henry Hailsham-Brown	JOHN WARWICK
Inspector Lord	CAMPBELL SINGER
Constable Jones	DESMOND LLEWELYN

The Play is directed by WALLACE DOUGLAS

Décor by MICHAEL WEIGHT

Margaret Lockwood, whom Desmond knew at RADA, is described as an absolute sweetie with an incredibly vulgar laugh. With her daughter, 'Toots', she became a frequent visitor to Chelsea Park Gardens and always managed to give Desmond's flagging confidence a terrific boost.

The Spiders Web also curtailed holidays in Ireland. Pamela, however, continued to spend a few weeks there in the summer with the boys and stayed at the holiday cottage owned by her mother in Co. Mayo. Left alone in London, Desmond occasionally sought the dubious attentions of a prostitute, which he insists with a dismissive twinkle was just a physical thing caused by absence. "I never wanted an affair. I adored Pamela far too much."

The relief of knowing the final weeks of *The Spiders Web* were imminent also brought disappointing news. With his hopes relegated to ashes, Desmond learned he'd been rejected for a role in *The Bridge on the River Kwai,* supposedly because he was not thin enough. This lame excuse bore a marked similarity to that offered in 1946 when he auditioned for a film about POWs and was turned down for being too old!

By 1957, the pleasures of living in London with two children had palled. It also became expensive and when offered £10,500, having only paid £4,500, for their house in Chelsea Park Gardens, Desmond and Pamela accepted, (regrettably with hindsight, as these properties sell for well over a million today). But the move to Battle in East Sussex was an obvious one. It was conveniently close to Pamela's parents. The children preferred the countryside and so for that matter did Desmond. Whitelands, the Georgian house they'd always coveted had come on the market reasonably cheaply and coincidentally at £4,500, which would provide a bit of extra cash to do the renovations.

With the move accomplished, a dearth of acting work left Desmond free to harass the builders and concentrate on decorating, until a few weeks employment at the Frinton Summer Theatre gave him a chance to direct a familiar play - *The Spiders Web* and appear in *Separate Tables.* Amongst the cast, professing to step nervously into her first role, was a teenage Vanessa Redgrave. "To think I had the good fortune to direct such wonderfully natural talent. In *The Spider's Web,* Vanessa took the part of the gardener, a role originally played by a butch friend, Judith Furse. As we had only a week's rehearsal, I pointed out where all the laughs were and how to get them. After a couple of days, Vanessa got fed up and asked to play the gardener her way, so I let her have a go. She was twice as brilliant and got twice as many laughs."

When the season was over, Desmond returned to his decorator's overalls and the serious task of getting Whitelands into shape. Friends who came to stay for a peaceful weekend were given a paint scraper and put to work. "My dears," uttered one as she left on the Sunday for the safety of London. "I don't know how you stand this mess, or the noise. If I lived here I'd shoot all those bloody birds that sing in the mornings!"

But the Llewelyns had no wish to return to the city as they discovered the pleasures of a rural environment. The Dean of Battle, Arthur Naylor, became a great friend of Desmond's and their circumspective thoughts on the last war often continued long into the night. "He was a jolly chap; got the DSO in spite of falling out with Montgomery. They had a row about brothels. Arthur wanted to close them all and Monty wanted to keep them open - probably felt his men would fight better if they'd been serviced."

After a tiny part in the film *Ivanhoe* (with Roger Moore), a surprise job for Welsh TV took Desmond to Cardiff for three weeks where the incomplete studio was still under construction within an old chapel. The producer proffered apologies. "There were no proper dressing rooms, nowhere to eat in comfort and I remember one chap was sitting on the loo when suddenly, the builder took the door away."

Rehearsing proved to be tricky as a number of the cast were amateurs and had other jobs during the day. Excuses such as funerals, audits or plumbing were commonplace. One amateur, however, was clearly considering becoming a full time actor. "Apart from your job, how much do you earn as an amateur?" queried somebody casually. "Around a couple of thousand a year," he replied. "Jesus Christ," yelped Desmond, leaping up. "That's twice as much as I earn and I'm a professional."

On and off throughout the 1950's, unemployment (with a capital 'U') provided the semblance of a job for one day a week. "Pamela used to get very cross with me when I told people I was going to the Labour Exchange to sign on. 'It's not so bad in London,' she'd say. 'But down here in Battle, people talk y'know.' So what, I'd reply. Everybody does it, even well-known actors."

In 1959, Desmond appeared in the well-loved TV series, *Dixon of Dock Green,* featuring Jack Warner as PC George Dixon; they'd previously met some years earlier at a show starring Tommy Trinder and Arthur Askey. One day Jack leaned confidentially across to Desmond and said, "Your hair's going grey and that's no good for business. Do what I do and put some colour on it." Grecian 2000 or the equivalent was quickly used to good effect - or so he thought. Ivor questioned him closely. "Daddy, why is your hair starting to turn ginger?"

For six weeks, Desmond succumbed to the joys of Ireland and being paid with a small role in *The Sword of Sherwood Forest.* The film itself left little impression except that his scene of galloping away on a horse followed by a volley of arrows and then falling to the ground, he accomplished without the aid of a stunt man. The evenings were spent in the company of the rest of the cast (including a young Oliver Reed) and plenty of Irish Whiskey. "Wonderful stuff. It had the advantage of dulling the knowledge that at forty-five, I was still playing 'bit' parts and knowing that, come the morning, I wouldn't have a hangover. Perhaps, as Pamela once suggested, I should have been a schoolmaster."

- 6 -

FROM RUSSIA WITH LOVE, GOLDFINGER AND THUNDERBALL

"Who'd have thought the Bond movies
would capture the world."

- 6 -
FROM RUSSIA WITH LOVE, GOLDFINGER AND THUNDERBALL

Blue skies, Rome and the epic production of *Cleopatra* introduced the sixties decade. The film, in its embryo stages, predicted to make millions, was fraught with problems from the outset; not least the leading lady, Elizabeth Taylor falling seriously ill. Nine months would pass before the doctors declared her fit to work again. Meanwhile, the extravagant sets built at Pinewood were torn down and hundreds of 'extras' dismissed as Joseph Mankiewicz took over the reins and re-wrote the script, now insisting that *Cleopatra* must be filmed in Rome - the grey skies of Pinewood were simply not conducive. To play opposite Elizabeth Taylor, Richard Burton, the Welsh miner's son with an unquenchable thirst for the limelight, had to be poached from his role in *Camelot*, costing Twentieth Century Fox an undisclosed fortune.

At the studios in Rome, sets were rebuilt, Italian 'extras' were hired, fired and hired again as the theatrical profession from various parts of the globe congregated around the nerve centre of Cleopatra's makers. A pseudo repertory company, consisting of about twenty British actors and actresses, had been established 'on site' to save flipping backwards and forwards to the UK when a small part suddenly arose.

Amongst this body of actors was Desmond. He had two parts - a soldier in the crowd scenes and a senator with just four lines. "I'd appeared in *Pirates of Blood River* and the same casting director was used for *Cleopatra*. I went out to Rome in September 1961 and apart from a two month break at Christmas, when I came home and fortunately got a part in *The 2nd Mrs. Tanqueray*, I stayed in Italy for nine months. It really was rather pleasant hanging around in such a beautiful city and being paid £50 a week.

Maddeningly, it could have been £500 a week, but little realising the Americans equated a high wage with better quality, it was suggested their offer was overly generous and in order to keep expenses down £50 would be more than enough. The Italians soon caught on to the American willingness to pay through the nose, misguidedly assuming it assured the best goods. For instance, when horses were needed, the production company was offered the best animals at a substantially inflated price having been informed horses were expensive at this time of the year. When it came to selling the same beasts, heads were shaken and hands wrung; the bottom had fallen out of the market; it was almost impossible to sell horses unless they were very cheap!"

This one small example partially illustrates why the costs and problems on *Cleopatra* snowballed as those on the payroll enjoyed themselves. Most, including Desmond, fell into the routine of going to the studios in the morning, having a free lunch on set and spending the afternoon sightseeing, riding or going to concerts.

Finally, the day arrived for 'Senator Desmond's' four short lines which followed a long speech by Roddy McDowell, who played Octavius. "I practised my piece to perfection as I waited for poor old Roddy who fluffed his discourse time after time. It took the entire morning before he eventually got it right and then disaster - I made a cock-up of my meagre words. Oh the shame: never have I been so miserably embarrassed. I apologised to Roddy who was extremely kind and told me not worry; he didn't mind doing his speech again. Then I went over to Jo Mankiewicz and

Desmond as one of the Roman soldiers in *Cleopatra*. Rome 1967.

apologised. "My dear chap," he said, looking at me pityingly. "I wouldn't have been in your shoes for anything."

The well publicized scandal of the affair between Richard Burton and Elizabeth Taylor added yet another complication to the production, particularly as each had their respective partners with them. Desmond had known fellow Welshmen, Richard, and his brother, Ifor (also in Rome), for some years. Elizabeth, he met for the first time when dining with other members of the cast at a club-cum-restaurant near the Spanish Steps. As he got up to go to the Gents, a familiar voice sounded in his ear. It was Richard, with Elizabeth sitting at a nearby table. "He introduced her to me and we chatted for a bit. I could see why he fell for her, she really was fiendishly divine. I remember glancing across that thick sheen of black hair and, through the window, seeing the paparazzi swarming like flies outside the restaurant. I suggested to Richard, if discretion was paramount and they wished to leave unnoticed, why not let Elizabeth put a head scarf on and slip out of the back door with me. He seemed to think it was a good idea, but indicated neither were ready - yet. My plan came to nothing when two hours later they made a grand exit together, amidst cameras, flashlights and questions. From this, I deduced that in spite of denials, they loved all the attention. Even so, when the going got tough, Richard sometimes made a heartfelt plea to me. 'For Christ's sake, you're a Welshman, too, can't you take her off my hands?' I was very tempted."

In March, Pamela's mother, who had been ill with cancer, died and Desmond flew home for the funeral, afterwards returning to Rome to finish filming. Later, Pamela joined him for a few days and one evening they dined with Richard and Elizabeth. The latter had the reputation of being able to charm anybody regardless of sex or age and she left Pamela in total agreement with her husband. Elizabeth was divine and as they'd both spent most of the evening discussing caesarian births, she felt it had been like chatting to the girl next door.

With a magnificent fanfare the premiere of *Cleopatra* brought the film to its deliciously scandalous, star packed and costly conclusion. Now it desperately needed to earn some cash.

Around the same time and with far less fuss, another film caught the public's attention. *Dr. No* (1962) was the baby of producers Harry Saltzman and Cubby Broccoli, a movie based on an Ian Fleming thriller about the secret agent, James Bond 007. It proved sensational and rapidly showed enough profit to guarantee a second Bond film *From Russia With Love.*

The rather unlikely partnership of Saltzman and Broccoli only occurred because of Ian Fleming's puzzling agreement (although it has been suggested he needed the money for medical bills) to sell an option on all his 007 books, except *Casino Royale*, to film maker Harry Saltzman. In turn, producer Cubby Broccoli had read Fleming's James Bond thrillers and was convinced his books could be made into highly successful action-packed films. When he subsequently discovered Saltzman owned the rights, he arranged to have him invited to his office for a meeting. Within hours, the virtual strangers had hashed out the superficial problems and agreed to co-produce the films on a fifty-fifty basis, calling their company EON (Everything Or Nothing) Productions.

At the beginning of 1963, Desmond's agent, Mary Harris, phoned him with the offer of one day's work on the second Bond film *From Russia With Love*. Was he interested? Of course he was interested. Whilst Welsh TV had been fairly lucrative since *Cleopatra*, the promises of: 'got just the part coming up for you' made by sundry moguls in Rome, had come to nothing.

From Russia with Love is suggested to be the most serious, least spectacular and yet one of the best Bond films. The setting is Istanbul and the first class plot involves murder, blackmail, beautiful women, a hazardous train journey aboard the Orient Express and a selective mix of lethal villains, all anxious to annihilate 007. Sean Connery plays James Bond to his full advantage and with the help of gadgets from Q Branch, outwits the entire bunch of gangsters from the criminal organisation S.P.E.C.T.R.E (The Special Executive for Counter-Intelligence, Terrorism, Revenge and Extortion). Led by Ernst Stavro Blofeld, this outfit re-appears in several more Bond films.

Q Branch is an abbreviation of Quartermaster's Stores, and this is where the derivation of the Secret Service code initial Q begins to emerge as a pseudonym for Boothroyd - although it remains Major Boothroyd in the credits until the fourth film, *Thunderball.*

The official armourer, Major Boothroyd of Q branch, had been played in *Dr. No* by Peter Burton. Fortunately for Desmond, he was unavailable for filming the second Bond. Remembering his Welsh accent from *Divided* days, director Terence Young asked Desmond, when he arrived at Pinewood studios, how he envisaged portraying Boothroyd. In reply to Desmond's, "Just kind of straight," Terence shook his head. "I want you to play him as a Welshman." Desmond strongly disagreed. "It won't work Terence; Boothroyd needs to be a toffee-nosed Englishman, not a broad Welshman." A heated argument ensued until Desmond proved his point by launching forth into the thickest Welsh dialogue possible. Terence capitulated immediately.

In *Dr. No*, Major Boothroyd is responsible for getting 007 to replace his Beretta 22 for a Walther PPK. This actual oversight in Fleming's original writing was corrected by a genuine guns expert from Glasgow, Geoffrey Boothroyd. He wrote to Fleming thus:-

> 'I like everything about your James Bond except his deplorable taste in weapons. A Beretta 22 is utterly useless as well as being a ladies gun - and not a very nice lady at that!'

Until then, Fleming, a former Naval Intelligence officer, had paid little attention to 007 survival equipment. Realising he needed to rectify this error, he introduced an arms expert named Major Boothroyd into his next book.

The producers liked the impression of the inaugural encounter between 007 and Boothroyd so much, they decided to effect another meeting in *From Russia With Love*. By then, Boothroyd's knowledge of equipment had increased tenfold as he became head of the division that supplies Bond with gadgets and Desmond played him in the straightforward manner of an aristocratic senior technician. He first entered the action when M (head of the British Secret Service) requests Miss Moneypenney - whilst 007 is in the office - to ask Major Boothroyd to come in. "Hang on, we can't do that," interjected Terence. "Let's change it to 'ask the equipment officer to come in. Q Branch has got together a nice looking piece of luggage'."

"Unforgettable" is the way Desmond describes his first day on Bond. It started with a difference when producer, Cubby Broccoli, welcomed him in person to the Pinewood studio; an unusual occurrence and, for a small part actor, unheard of. "Cubby was one of the nicest, most thoughtful men I have ever met; one warmed to him immediately and instinctively I knew if I had any problems he'd always help." The meeting resulted in a long, if spasmodic, friendship.

Cubby's informal and friendly manner evoked a similar empathy in others. His reputation for having a big-hearted personality drew a loyal following from most who worked with him. Possessing a colourful ancestry, he was the son of Giovanni and descended from the Italian Broccolis of Carrera whose claim to posterity was crossing Cauliflower and Rabi to produce the vegetable that took the family name. According to the records, around the turn of the century the Broccolis emigrated to the United States, where Giovanni eventually set up a small farming enterprise employing Cubby and his brother. After a series of agricultural disasters and the death of his father, Cubby went to stay with his rich cousin, Pat DeCicco, in California. With his 'salesman' abilities and his cousin's Hollywood contacts, Cubby found himself mingling with the top echelon of the movie world; before long he became fascinated by the business and gained valuable experience on a Howard Hughes production *The Outlaw*, in the early 1940's. When the war was over, Cubby continued his self-education in the film industry and in 1951 co-produced his first venture with Irving Allen, *The Red Beret*. Since then, he has never looked back.

On his only day of filming *From Russia With Love*, Desmond's companions (apart from the crew) were Sean Connery (007), Bernard Lee (M) and Lois Maxwell (Miss Moneypenny). With hindsight, his scene where, as the Equipment Officer, he walks into M's office carrying the now famous briefcase, must be the benchmark of his career. In clipped tones, he goes on to explain the idiosyncrasies of this insignificant piece of business luggage to 007:-

> "Here is an ordinary black leather case. Hidden in these steel rods are twenty rounds of ammunition. Press that button and you have a throwing knife. Inside is your AR7, a folding sniper's rifle and 50 gold sovereigns. This looks like an ordinary tin of talcum powder, but it conceals a tear gas cartridge and is kept in place by a magnetic device... Now, when you normally open a briefcase like this one, you move the catches from side to side. If you do that, the tear gas cartridge will explode in your face; instead, you must first turn the catches horizontally and then move them to the side..."

A rare photograph of Desmond's scene with 007 (Sean Connery) and M (Bernard Lee) in *From Russia With Love*

Bond, of course, is armed with other gadgets from the bounteous Q Branch, including a special Rolleiflex camera with a built in recording device and a bleeper to warn him of an incoming telephone call.

Many of the film's triumphs were undoubtedly due to director Terence Young, in himself an arch Bond type, always impeccably dressed, with a love of expensive living. It was Terence who groomed Sean Connery from his rough, tough Scot, ex-coffin polisher/milkman image, into the charismatic smoothie, 007; the built in sex appeal, however, belonged to Connery alone. It's suggested, when Terence first heard of Cubby's choice of Bond, he put his head in his hands and said, "Disaster, disaster, disaster." Fleming himself hoped for David Niven or Cary Grant.

Regretting his role couldn't be expanded, Desmond found his one day's work a fascinating experience from which he earned about £30 and met Ian Fleming for the first time when he joined the cast for drinks. "I asked him if he recollected a friend of mine being at school with him at Eton. He said, yes, but I don't suppose he did. After that, I didn't really think any more about the film. None of us, except perhaps Connery, were stars then and the Bond hype hadn't begun."

The screen version of Fleming's most classic thriller took the public by storm and *From Russia with Love* surpassed *Dr. No* in every aspect and drew crowds of ever increasing fans. As a newcomer with just a few words, Q's potential had not yet been realised and therefore Desmond did not get invited to the premiere. Unrecognised, he watched the film at his local cinema in Hastings.

Before returning to the TV studios in Cardiff, work, once again, went ominously quiet and Desmond, "got in some very satisfying decorating." In February 1964, he did a TV series *The Plane Makers*, before an unpleasant domestic incident occurred. At the time, he and Pamela were staying in London, having just met the boys from school. A telephone call late that night and the anxious voice of Pamela's father,

Charles, augured bad news. He informed them a part of Whitelands had been gutted by fire and although the fire brigade had contained the flames to one side of the house, the dining room and room above were badly damaged. "We felt so helpless, but Pamela remained remarkably controlled and having established the fire was well and truly extinguished, suggested there was no point in racing down to Battle in the pitch dark; we might as well wait until the next day. Too much wine at dinner that night might have had something to do with her decision."

Ten hours later, they stood outside Whitelands surveying the wreckage. On first impression it looked worse than originally assumed and the dining room had turned into a charred, ceilingless twelve foot void. Unsuspecting rafters gawped at the sodden shambles below. Fragments of curtain flapped absurdly against shattered windows. The chaos was indescribable.

The clearing up operation proved a thankless task, particularly as Desmond was called back to Cardiff for another TV play *Moulded in Earth*. "I did feel rather guilty leaving everything to Pamela, but I appeased my conscience a tiny bit by humping all the salvaged furniture to our local restorer, Mr. More, who had the honesty to admit he liked nothing better than a good fire to perk up business!"

By now, filming the third Bond *Goldfinger* had begun, but, frustratingly, Desmond had heard nothing from his agent. Instead, he accepted a part in TV's *Danger Man*, starring Patrick McGoohan. Coincidentally, this tough good looking six-footer was reputedly amongst the first actors approached to play 007. It's suggested he turned it down flatly, on the grounds the sex scenes were too explicit and as an ardent Catholic felt they were not conducive to family life.

The request to play Q in *Goldfinger* finally arrived, this time under the directorship of Guy Hamilton. According to Desmond, it was Guy's brilliant expertise that balanced the serious and the humourous side of James Bond to perfection. Guy was also responsible for changing Desmond's approach to Q.

"When the script arrived for *Goldfinger*, I had great difficulty in learning the lines. Somehow, they didn't fit in with a serious man talking about a lethal gadget. I soon learned why. Previously, I'd played Boothroyd as a toffee-nosed technician, a civil servant, more than slightly in awe of Bond. This manifested itself in the first rehearsal of *Goldfinger* when 007 comes into the room where I'm working at the desk and I stand up to greet him. Instantly, Guy called, 'No, no, no. Don't take any notice of him.' He said, 'This man annoys you. He's irritatingly flippant and doesn't treat your gadgets with respect. Deep down you may envy his charm with women, but remember you're the teacher and on no account should you stand up when he appears.' Guys few words provided a valuable critique and thereafter I played Q showing a veiled exasperation coupled with a humourous tolerance to 007's flippancy and aggravating habit of fiddling with the gadgets."

Regrettably, Desmond's part in *Goldfinger* was small and the few hours of filming took place again, at Pinewood, one Friday. On arriving home that evening, an urgent phone call awaited him. The voice of one of Guy's assistants echoed down the line. "Cubby wants you back again. We've decided to do an ejector seat scene and you're needed in the studios on Monday. O.K.?" Of course it was O.K. More work, more money.

However, Broccoli and Saltzman held differing opinions on this scene. Saltzman didn't want Q explaining the ejector seat, favouring instead to create surprise when it happened. Broccoli, on the other hand, felt if the audience were forewarned, it created the preferable element of suspense. "The set's still there. Let's get Desmond back, shoot the scene and decide afterwards," suggested Guy. They did, and suspense overruled surprise.

The Aston Martin DB5 featuring the saw blade. *Goldfinger*.

Little did Desmond realise how significant Monday's filming would be when the ejector seat sequence and his much quoted punch line, 'I never joke about my work 007,' firmly established his place in the growing Bond phenomena. These are the opening remarks to those seven words:-

Q: (curtly) "Oh, hello 007. This way please."

007: "Where's my Bentley?" (as he walks across the warehouse).

Q: "We've got a new car. The old one was becoming unreliable."

007: "Never let me down yet."

Q: "From now on you'll be using this Aston Martin DB5. (He then runs his hand over the car and stops)... Now at the top of the gearstick you'll find a little red button. Whatever you do don't touch it."

007: "Why not?"

Q: "If you do you'll release a section of the roof and engage, then fire the ejector seat."

007: "You're joking."

Q: (exasperated at being taken so lightly replies) "I NEVER joke about my work 007."

Desmond's scenes, mainly with Connery, were completed in two days. He never did get to meet the leading ladies; 9 carat gold Shirley Eaton or Honor Blackman, who played judo expert Pussy Galore. Nor did he ever set eyes on the film's latest villain, Auric Goldfinger. This role was played by German actor, Gert Frobe, whose capacity for the English language encompassed: 'good morning', 'plissed to mit you' and little else. Not a problem according to Guy. By getting Gert to speak the lines fairly quickly in his native lingo, his voice was superbly dubbed by Michael Collins.

Sadly, 007's creator, Ian Fleming, died on 1st August 1964, just over a month before the screen version of *Goldfinger*, written in 1959, had its premiere. He was fifty-six.

Released in September 1964, the film broke all previous records and became a box office success. The highly improbable tale about the avaricious Goldfinger endeavouring to destroy all the gold in Fort Knox in order to boost his own bullion, epitomised the pure escapism, glamour and fantasy of Bond and it hit the mid 60s public at just the right time.

When Fleming was once asked, "What constitutes a good thriller?" He suavely replied, "to any thriller add all the advantages of expensive living, then give the hero (in this case James Bond) the right background and beautiful women. Set the tale in the most romantic of places and take it along so fast that nobody will notice its idiosyncrasies." The producers obliged and thrill follows thrill so quickly there is no time for analysis. Tension is eased by humour and the sure knowledge that Bond will win in the end. Even Auric Goldfinger's sidekick, Oddjob, the meanest of villains with an unnerving habit of flinging his steel rimmed bowler hat at people with deadly accuracy is no match for 007.

The emergence of the priceless Aston Martin DB5 in *Goldfinger* is shown filled with elaborate defence mechanisms. Set to be the longest lasting Bond gadget, it was either updated or replaced in subsequent films. No one item has been so revered; from schoolboys upwards, they all adored this erotic piece of machinery stuffed with high tech nonsense. Or, is it? This first Aston Martin supplied by Q branch is the subject of many of Desmond's talks on Bond and he puts a different perspective on the whole caboodle.

"Apart from desirability, what is remarkable about an Aston Martin? Nothing, unless it belongs to 007. Naturally, it will have revolving number plates - a device dreamed up by Guy who was having problems with parking tickets. Next come the electrically operated tyre shredders that appear from the wheel hubs. These were used on the chariots in *Ben Hur*; that's where the idea stemmed from. Water cannons; the European police have those. Oil slicks were favoured by the 1930's gangsters and the ejector seat is not really remarkable at all; aeroplanes have had them for years. What's brilliant is combining the whole lot in one car and you're so carried away by excitement or laughter, you don't have time to think: where the hell is all the oil, water and petrol stored?"

Hot on the heels of *Goldfinger* came *Thunderball*. Whilst still undergoing its initial development, Desmond played a jailer in the film *Moll Flanders*. Shot at Shepperton Studios and on location at Chilham Castle, several days appeared to be taken up with the aforementioned jailer dragging the leading lady from cell to cell, "Whilst she fought like hell." During a quiet moment, he challenged *Moll Flanders* director, the recognizable Terence Young. "I hear you're directing *Thunderball*. Will I be needed as Major Boothroyd again?" Predictably, he just shrugged his shoulders and said, "Haven't got a clue."

The history of *Thunderball* was somewhat topsy-turvy. The original story had been a film script, co-written for a recently formed film company, by Ian Fleming and Kevin McClory with screen writer Jack Wittingham. Their film flopped. Nobody wanted Bond. "Who the hell would be interested in a Limey detective?" said the Americans. Subsequently, Ian Fleming re-wrote the script into a James Bond novel. When McClory read an advanced copy, he realised a large amount of it was his and Jack Wittingham's work. He sued and the plumped out wrangling that followed fattened the legal hierarchy and McClory eventually won all the film and TV rights to *Thunderball*. Initially, Saltzman and Broccoli had planned to shoot *Thunderball* as the first Bond instead of *Dr. No*, but the legal complications halted the go-ahead by three years; a sobering indication of just how long litigation had been simmering. The final outcome was a tepid merger with Kevin McClory becoming the Producer and Broccoli and Saltzman the Presenters.

Kevin's input had a fairly important bearing on Desmond for three reasons. Firstly, and simply, they got on very well. Secondly, it was during Kevin's reign that the conventional Major Boothroyd tag was firmly replaced with the unconventional Q and thirdly, he invited Desmond and Pamela to the Royal Premiere of *Thunderball* as his guests, unknowingly establishing a future precedence.

At Pinewood, the shooting of *Thunderball* incurred a few hitches and Desmond hung around the studios waiting to deliver Q's brief on various devices. Somehow it never happened and as the cast were due to film in the Bahamas for the next few weeks, he assumed his scene would be done on their return.

That evening, a phone call informed him otherwise. "Get your bags packed. You're flying out to the Bahamas tomorrow. Q's scene is needed for wet weather cover and we're building a special set." Pamela understandably complained. "Whenever the boys break up from school, you go off somewhere." There was another reason too. The year before, she'd inherited 'Linkwell', her mother's ancestral home, a Georgian property lying a few miles south of Battle, at Bexhill-on-Sea. Unfortunately, the splendid stuccoed appearance of Linkwell belied its poor condition, both internally and externally. Substantial repairs were essential before occupation.

For many years it had been owned by Pamela's uncle who harboured a curious loathing for the place. He refused to live in it and barely set foot across the parqueted threshold, choosing instead to make his home in the adjacent gardener's cottage. By then, the already neglected Linkwell had twice been used as a school and then converted to bedsits. Sadly down marketed, it was hard to visualise the 18th century residence as it had once been - a place where visiting gentry stepped from horse drawn carriages to be shown by a waiting, liveried servant into a gracefully proportioned interior.

Even Desmond's normally ebullient personality showed distinct signs of apprehension at the upheaval. "The building had bomb damage; the roof had leaked into most of the upstairs rooms; there was rising damp, antiquated plumbing, the entire place had been painted urinal green and it was freezing." Small wonder Pamela complained. Builders, plumbers and Desmond's general navvying and decorating abilities had been harnessed weeks in advance of their forthcoming move into Linkwell. Now it would all have to be re-organised due to, in Pamela's own words: "That bloody Bond rubbish."

In truth, Pamela hardly ever bitched and bore her husband's itinerant career with the tolerance of a detached auntie. Desmond defends her slip of the tongue. "She really was totally supportive. But having realised I'd never be the schoolmaster she aspired to marry, she hoped I'd dig up enough ability to pursue classical acting with a degree of success." A forlorn hope. Pamela had to put up with Bond instead.

March 1965. 102 actors and technicians plus 12 tons of equipment flew to Nassau in the Bahamas. The tiny island was about to witness as much disruption as an opulent hurricane. Even the islanders' annual carnival had been specifically re-arranged to be incorporated in a *Thunderball* scene where an injured 007 bears the hallmark of distinct uncertainty as he endeavours to lose his pursuers amongst the chanting, vividly dressed throng of dancing natives. Neither was the flight winging Desmond to the Bahamas entirely uneventful, for it necessitated a change of aircraft in New York. As Desmond had no visa, he was literally smuggled, Bond- style, from plane to airport to plane by armed guard, before landing on the Bahamas melting tarmac strip. The

"They really gave me the most hideous shirt to wear in *Thunderball*."

shimmering vista sweltered under acrylic blue skies and permanent sunshine. "Frankly, the prospect of rain looked about as likely as British Rail being on time."

The production manager, a fussy little man, cautioned him. "Whatever you do, stay out of the sun. We can't have you getting a tan. And don't leave the hotel without telling us first." Apart from avoiding a tan, Desmond soon discovered another unforseen problem. "What the hell do you talk about when the weather's perpetually brilliant?"

Waiting in the shade for the rain can be a fairly boring existence and in spite of being paid around £400 a week, including subsistence, Desmond was restless. He'd rehearsed Q's lines until they were perfect and simply being a spectator on the set of *Thunderball* became understandably frustrating.

He discovered a scrooge-like pleasure in eking out his subsistence by having a huge breakfast at the hotel, lunch on location and, if possible, an invitation for the evening. One early breakfast taken with a fellow actor, Earl Cameron, has been wedged in reachable memory. On this occasion his companion caught sight of an obvious friend and hailed him to join them for coffee. With some surprise, Desmond found himself being introduced to Martin Luther King. The ensuing conversation left an impressive imprint, yet, maddeningly, and here the blame is laid on advancing years, he cannot remember what the hell it was all about, except, "Luther King was utterly fascinating. I can still hear his voice, but not what he said."

A slight diversification, but one that evoked a similar feeling, reminded Desmond of Rome. Although he has never embraced Catholicism, he found a visit to St. Peter's Square to see the Pope engulfed him in a powerful aura. An audience with the illustrious man promised fulfilment of a youthful desire. Sadly, it never took place. The Vatican informed Desmond on his arrival that the Pope was too ill to see anybody. His death was announced a couple of days later.

"The Pope had been on my list of 'great men' and I'd certainly include Cubby in that. Maybe it had something to do with his caring attitude, his ability to transpose what he applied to Bond to everyday life. In his book, nothing was impossible and having daily contact with him throughout *Thunderball*, I became doubly aware of his kindness."

The suspense in *Thunderball* starts early, with the hijacking of a NATO bomber that eventually comes to grief on the floor of the ocean. As much of the action revolves around its watery resting place, there are a goodly number of none too friendly sharks and rubber clad villains to keep up the tension. The rest of the film is situated amongst tropical scenery, glittering pools (some revealing the intermittent movements of sharks), glasses clinking with ice cubes, veiled attempts on 007's life and a handful of ravishing semi-dressed women. The seductive Aston Martin DB5, now an integral part of Bond's life, also makes another appearance.

It's suggested that hundreds of actresses, including Julie Christie, Raquel Welch and Faye Dunaway auditioned for the coveted female role of Domino. It went to Claudine Auger, a French actress; Desmond is not shy when describing her, "She was terrific, electrifying and breathtakingly stunning."

Does he recollect feeling a trifle guilty when he compared Pamela's existence to his own at this point? "Well, yes." Then, "No, dammit, it was work." Changing the subject, he becomes expansive about one of Q's favourite *Thunderball* gadgets, the underwater camera. "This was the prototype of the modern camera. In the sixties, there were no small underwater cameras, but Nikon were working on the idea. When they learned such a device was needed for a Bond film it arrived by return of post!"

"Watching Sean film some of the shark scenes proved to be an eye-opener. It was the only time I saw him visibly scared; in spite of Terence's reassurances of the strong plastic corridor constructed across an expanse of water between him and certain death. I remember him saying to Sean, 'Look the only way the sharks can get you is

Q's very first publicity photo

Leaning on a set of aqualungs Bond demands an explanation of the specially equipped underwater camera. An exasperated Q gives instructions for the second time.

if they jump over the top like dolphins.' Sean replied, 'How the fuck do you know they don't?' I felt an enormous sympathy for Sean, he really did live under a microscope. Both fans and press pursued him relentlessly. Apparently, he gave only one interview during the entire making of *Thunderball*, curiously for *Playboy* magazine."

Entreaties to the rain gods made little difference as Q waited patiently in the shade, willing the odd cloud to precipitate a downpour. None came. His workshop scenery, completed a day or so after his arrival, gathered dust. The clothes (not his own this time) hung limply on a hanger. That Friday, he had a phone call from the production office, "It's obvious the weather ain't gonna change, so we've booked you a flight back home on Monday."

Uncertain whether to be glad or sad at the prospect of returning home, Desmond finished packing before going for a final swim. As he did so, the sky darkened, spots of rain fell and the phone rang. "Thank God you haven't gone. Cubby's going mad. You're needed on location. It's raining."

In the event, the rain turned out to be a fleeting offering and by the time he'd reached the set, it had stopped. Nevertheless, those few drops ensured a paid-up stay in the Bahamas for the entire duration of filming. His scene was eventually shot at Pinewood on their return in May where in his reconstructed workshop and clad in an uncharacteristic highly coloured shirt, Q tells 007 'to be a little less than his usual frivolous self' as Bond makes a throwaway remark and plonks his hat on top of the underwater equipment. Q then hands 007 a minute piece of sub-aqua breathing apparatus and a red flare saying: "This is to be kept on you at all times in case of emergency." Sadly, he doesn't demonstrate the zippy Bell-Textron rocket belt, a one man piece of flying machinery used by 007 to escape from a chateau, the French home of Jacques Boitier, a S.P.E.C.T.R.E. killer. The Bell Textron jump jet was first spotted by an EON associate in a demonstration film made to sell the unit to the U.S. military as a quick escape device for Commandos. "The whole scene was filmed in a very posh Parisian suburb," said Desmond, "and I've always had a mental picture of some businessman gazing out of the window and seeing a man flying past with no visible means of support. It certainly would have sent him rushing off for his brandy decanter."

Swapping six star warmth for a chilly barn-like place undergoing restoration, took a bit of getting used to. In his absence, Pamela had successfully bullied the builders. The bedsitter basins adorning most rooms were gone. The skeleton of a central heating system had been put in place. Fireplaces were being re-instated. A kitchen ordered from Ideal Home had arrived. "All that remained was the physical relocation into Linkwell's chaos, plus redecoration of the entire place, which was down to me."

The move into Linkwell was completed in the summer and some weeks later, whilst Desmond was still clad in overalls and paint, Pamela came into the room. "Kevin McClory's on the phone. He wants to talk to you. He's asking us to go to the premiere of *Thunderball* as his guests."

As 1965 drew to a close, the largest crowd yet stood outside the Odeon Leicester Square, waiting for the stars of the latest Bond to arrive for the Royal Premiere. They were not disappointed. One by one, two by two and car by car they came: walking a short circuit to acknowledge the cheers. Heady stuff for Desmond, who, with his pleasure apparent at first time recognition, waved before going inside with Pamela to watch the finished production of *Thunderball*.

The film, one of his favourites, does not come without his criticism. "I find one of the killing scenes in rather bad taste; the villain is thrown to the sharks and the water turns blood red. Again, in the much later film, *Licence to Kill*, some poor guy is shoved into a decompression chamber and through the glass door you see the bits and pieces

In France filming the rocket belt enabling 007 to make a quick getaway to the awaiting Aston Martin. *Thunderball*.

going round. Killing, Bond-style, should be and usually is, done gracefully. No blood and gore. For example, again in *Thunderball*, 007 shoots somebody in the stomach with a spear gun, then says, 'I think he's got the point' and everybody roars with laughter."

Q's scene was, as usual, brief. In fact, the editor, Peter Hunt, had the temerity to dispense with most of it. Not Q's fault. "We didn't like the other chap who appeared with you," said Peter, "so we cut it out altogether. However, we've got some smashing shots of you when we let the cameras roll on afterwards and we've joined the bits together and used those instead."

These very shots, impromptu and unrehearsed, earned Q his first reviews for a James Bond movie.

007 wearing the Bell-Textron rocket belt.

- 7 -

A DOUBLE LIFE

'Little Nellie' ***You Only Live Twice.***

"All the gadgets are prototypes.
Just bigger and better than the inventor
originally made them."

- 7 -
A DOUBLE LIFE

Slowly Linkwell took shape, bit by bit, regaining its former Georgian graciousness as the years of neglect were stripped away. Desmond was in his element as he tackled the mammoth task of decorating a six bedroomed property after the builders had completed the structural work. Unfortunately, the kitchen units, purchased from Ideal Home, looked ghastly in situ and had to be removed, re-packed and sent back. "Nobody appeared to mind very much and we didn't have to pay."

One outstanding feature was the beautiful, but neglected, garden, rolling away to the south with extensive views of the sea. This was flanked by great banks of unpruned Rhododendrons, trees and weeds, some waist high. It cried out for attention and as soon as a degree of order reigned within the house, Desmond turned his abilities to the surrounding grounds. Perhaps it was just as well he had no acting commitments at that point in time.

With his talent for navvying in full swing, he ruthlessly pruned the trees and shrubs, cut down the weeds, forked over flower beds and, at Pamela's instigation, dug a huge vegetable garden. As a house warming present, Charles had paid for the instalment of a glamorous kidney- shape swimming pool. "Which cost a fortune to run, but partially made up for leaving Whitelands." Pamela had no regrets. She'd been born in the upstairs rooms at Linkwell and had now completed the full circle. She adored the place and was content to follow the traditions of her predecessors.

Linkwell.

Over the next few years, Desmond endeavoured to grasp the 'ins' and 'outs' of market gardening as he worked for long hours in the outsize vegetable patch or the netted cage (which he built himself) filled with soft fruit. "We were entirely self-sufficient. Any surplus I'd sell to the local greengrocer. It made me angry when friends commented: 'Oh, you're always on holiday'. I'd tell them, 'I'm not on bloody holiday. If you must know I'm working a damned sight harder than if I were doing a film'." Both Ivor and Justin are sceptical about their father's gardening abilities. They only recall him digging voraciously and trying to inject new life into unwilling soil. His fixation with fertilizing his vegetable garden left Justin mortified when he borrowed his father's car to take a girlfriend to the cinema. As he opened the car door, a great pong engulfed them from the back seat, where bags of rotting, stinking chicken shit had lain since Desmond had collected them from a farm three days earlier. "Locally, I was known as the manure man and I even stopped on the way to Pinewood to collect free horse shit from a stables. On one occasion, I went to the studios and discovered some elephant's dung from an elephant they were using in a film - it was jolly good!"

By the time the fifth Bond *You Only Live Twice* had been released, the dry down-to-earth interchanges between Q and 007 were an established feature. Desmond had added some valuable flesh to Q's character, even though his brief scenes gave little scope for development. These were mostly on a one to one basis with 007, although sometimes M, played by old friend Bernard Lee, made an appearance. "He was a delightful character who usually faced the day fortified by several large Scotches or a bottle of gin. Barely able to stand up, he'd be in front of the cameras, swaying slightly, yet the minute they rolled into action, he'd be word perfect and his acting would be immaculate. When the cameras cut, he'd practically pass out. It's said - I don't know how true it is - that when his house burned down, he was so tight, he didn't even notice."

Much of the shooting for *You Only Live Twice* took place in Japan and, in spite of reservations, Desmond flew there for a few days in the summer of 1966. His initial doubts were quickly dispelled after a superb flight over the Pole with first class comforts, ending with an efficient transfer to 'the most wonderful hotel in Tokyo'. Dining early on exquisite food, having eased his travel weary body into a warm bath, afforded the luxury of an early night - until the phone rang. It was Tom Carlile, the American representative of U.I.P. (United Independent Pictures), asking him out to a nightclub. "Many thanks old chap, but I'm much too tired and anyway, I'm in my pyjamas." Desmond replied. "To hell with that," said the voice down the line. "This is Tokyo. Go downstairs, have a Turkish bath and a massage and you'll find you can stay up all night. See you in an hour."

The star gadget of *You Only Live Twice*, a tiny auto gyrocopter, christened 'Little Nellie', arrived on location one Sunday lunchtime. Q was there to welcome what he initially thought was a lawnmower in full flight, as she buzzed in like a proverbial blue-bottle. In the film, Q transports 'Little Nellie' to Japan, flat-packed in four mock-croc suitcases, and then proceeds to slot her together in front of a waiting James Bond, who had previously requested her help to reconnoitre a volcanic mountain where plans were afoot to launch an interceptor space rocket. "Is my little girl ready, yet?" he asks impatiently. Q, weary from his arduous travels, replies crossly, "Now look here 007 - I've had a long, tiring journey." Then with the customary essence of concealed irritation, he explains 'Little Nellies' attributes:- two rocket launchers firing heat-seeking air-to-air missiles, two flame throwers with a range of 80 yds, two machine guns, two smoke ejectors, aerial mines and a flight helmet containing a camera. For once, all went smoothly; no stumbling, no prompts, no mistakes and no distractions. "Cut, well done," called the director. "Excuse me," piped up a voice, "but as Mr. Llewelyn said his lines, he pointed out all the wrong gadgets!"

Q explaining the attributes of 'Little Nellie' to 007.

Interestingly, 'Little Nellie' was not just a seductive and fictitious result of the producers imagination, but a copy of the prototype designed and flown in *You Only Live Twice* by Wing Commander Kenneth H. Wallis at the beginning of the 1960's. Subsequently, both Ken Adam (production designer) and Harry Saltzman read about the amazing mini helicopter and both had the same thought: 'let's use that in a Bond film'. Yet, in spite of 'Little Nellie's' marvellous statistics (she was under 10 ft. long, had a top speed of 180 miles per hour, weighed 250 pounds and was capable of lifting twice that amount), she was never exploited in practise to her fullest capacity, even after the colourful eulogy of her accomplishments by Q.

Released in June 1967, the obvious difficulties of producing one blockbuster sensation after another, showed itself with *You Only Live Twice*. Trying to repeat the highly successful *Thunderball*, was almost inevitably an impossibility. Even the change in the line-up of the main crew (essential to retain fresh ideas) couldn't quite capture the triumphs of the last film. Sean too, was restless. Whilst a complete professional on screen, off screen, he was disenchanted with his 'Bond image', afraid of getting typecast and utterly pissed off with being followed everywhere by the paparazzi. He was adamant; Broccoli and Saltzman must find another 007 for their next movie. In a way, Desmond couldn't blame him for the decision, although he acknowledges, "Sean did get a bit bloody minded about the role that made him a star, although personally, I'd found him very patient to work with, even when I forgot my lines."

It was a time of change for everyone, including Desmond, who woke a slumbering Pamela at dawn complaining of acute indigestion. She, certain he was exaggerating, patted him on the head, murmured, 'poor darling, take some Milk of Magnesia' and went back to sleep, only to be re-awoken minutes later by Desmond in extreme pain. She called the doctor and he prescribed rest. Some hope! Still feeling oddly breathless, but careless of his health as usual, Desmond insisted he went to London that same morning for a camera rehearsal. Feeling marginally better, he stayed the night at his father-in-law's flat, but on returning home next day experienced difficulty in running for the train and nearly collapsed in the carriage. At Pamela's instigation, he took the precautionary measure of visiting a specialist who diagnosed a heart attack, told him he was bloody lucky to be alive and, ignoring his protests, advised him to go home and stay in bed for six weeks. It was nearly three months before he was given the all clear to go back to work.

Screened in 1968, *Chitty Chitty Bang Bang* was a rollicking children's film based on the antics of a magic car. Curiously, the story was written by Ian Fleming shortly before he died and shows an unusual dimension to the character of the man famous for knife-edged thrillers. On Ian's death, Cubby Broccoli acquired the rights to *Chitty Chitty Bang Bang* and is said to have had great joy in producing such a delightful film starring the irrepressible Dick Van Dyke and Sally Ann Howes. Several familiar faces from Bond appeared in the production and amongst them Desmond had one day's work as the farmer who owned the car. Whilst on CCBB, he heard a story that illustrated one of Fleming's reputed eccentricities, but contradicted his written passion for strong arm tactics. "Whether it was true or not I don't know, but this chap had stayed with Fleming at his place in Jamaica and was horrified to discover giant bush rats scurrying around inside. At a loss to know what to do about these abhorrent inmates, he called a servant and suggested they should be exterminated. 'Commander Fleming dislikes any form of violence and will not have them killed. He says they can't help being bush rats,' explained the poker-faced servant, as though this justified the intrusion of the unwelcome house guests."

On Her Majesty's Secret Service (1969), but before filming could begin, it was necessary to find a new James Bond; a daunting task after the idolization bestowed on Sean Connery's 007. It was Cubby who discovered the Australian, George Lazenby, ex-car salesman and model, currently working on a few adverts. Lazenby had that same sexy, walk-tall attitude of Connery and although he had no acting experience, the choice, certainly on Cubby's part, seemed a forgone conclusion. Uncertain what was expected of him, even at the screen test, Lazenby stepped into the coveted shoes of 007, and within a short time the unknown actor pronounced himself a star - therein lay his downfall.

By all accounts, *On Her Majesty's Secret Service* should have been one of the most successful Bonds; the ingredients were perfect - almost. Desmond takes up the story. "It was one of Fleming's best tales; it had a brilliant director, Peter Hunt, and equally brilliant editor, John Glen; one of the best scriptwriters; a terrific cast (Diana Rigg and Telly Savalas) and some thrilling action shots in the Alps - George Lazenby was the fly in the ointment. He buggered the whole thing up by behaving like a sulky Prima Donna, both on and off screen. He wanted Bond-style attention all the time and it caused Cubby a lot of problems. Shame really, he may not have been Sean Connery, but he had his own brand of charisma and played 007, I thought, very adequately. He could have gone a long way if only he'd behaved himself. The cast really did get quite depressed about his churlish manner; he even walked off the set at 11.00 in the morning ostensibly because he wasn't allowed to ride a horse. Anyway, Cubby threw an impromptu party to cheer everybody up, which it did except for George, who sat glowering in the corner on his own. Cubby went over and said, 'Why don't you come and join us, what's the matter?' To which he replied, 'I should have had a proper invitation to this party, I'm the star.' 'Look George, the party evolved on the spur of the moment, nobody had an invitation, and just remember, you're not a star till the public makes you one,' said Cubby walking away."

Desmond, George Lazenby and Diana Rigg in 007's wedding scene from *On Her Majesty's Secret Service*.

In this film, Q's gadgets are almost non-existent; so is his presence. There is a fleeting scene fairly early on with M as he hands him a small object containing radio-active fluff, for use as a tracking device, then he disappears. Later, when the unlikely event of James Bond's marriage occurs, Q is on hand to offer his congratulations and also to remind him: 'If you need anything...' With a smile, 007 cuts across saying, 'Thanks Q, but I've got all the equipment - and I know how to use it'.

From memory, Desmond recalls the next couple of years being amongst his leanest. Auditions proved unproductive and he confessed to being fed up with struggling for recognition. Some radio and TV appearances in *Honey Lane, Its All In The Game, Love Story* with Ann Todd and *Virgin of The Secret Service*, saved his morale from a complete nose-dive. Luckily, a long hot summer also helped keep analytical reflections at bay as the impending drought required hours of watering shrivelling vegetables and wilting flowers. As always, Pamela provided the important mainstay, propping up Desmond's gregarious personality and discreetly ensuring he was kept occupied. Ivor and Justin, when at home, offered a distraction. "I think by then Ivor was at university reading something obscure like 'Norse' and Justin thought he, too, might like to become an actor, provided he could start at the top."

1971 and the corner turned ("But I'd turned so many corners.") as Desmond chalked up several appearances in TV's long running programme *Doomwatch*. Here, he was able to offer first hand advice to the leading man on 'how to have a heart attack and survive'. This coincided with landing the choice role as the benevolent Colonel in *Follyfoot*, a new children's series from Yorkshire Television. Inspired by the author Monica Dickens, great grand-daughter of Charles Dickens, the story is based loosely around the rather moody young Dora coming to stay with her uncle, a landowning Colonel, who is not short of a bob or two and runs a farm for rescued horses. The part suited Desmond to perfection. His genuine love of animals and his skill at handling horses, left over from childhood, required no acting; it was second nature.

The prestigious series, planned to run for three years, consisted of thirty-nine instalments both filmed and televised, in three separate stretches. In June 1971, YTV's first episode of *Follyfoot* gave, as one newspaper quoted, 'young viewers half an hour of sheer enchantment, surpassing most adult entertainment.' Apart from Desmond, the regulars featured Arthur English, prince of the wideboys in the 1950's, whose role as Slugger in *Follyfoot* was particularly appropriate as his father was a professional jockey and Arthur was literally brought up amongst horses. Gillian Blake, a young actress, played Dora who becomes closely attached to Copper, her handsome Arab stallion that makes his appearance towards the end of the first series. Steve Hodson as Steve and Christian Rodska as Ron Stryker completed the everyday residents of *Follyfoot*, which was shot at a reconstructed farmhouse on the Earl of Harewoods estate in Yorkshire.

Pamela with their two corgis at Linkwell

Although not yet typecast as Q, throughout the summer the critics wrote some favourable, if quizzical reviews on

Q is informed he must accompany 007 to Las Vegas.

Follyfoot's Colonel. *The Telegraph* reckoned, 'Desmond Llewelyn looks every inch a farmer as he strides around in his sensible country clothes'. Another wrote, 'The Squire certainly looks at home when he rides through the peace and tranquillity of the Yorkshire countryside'. Other headlines questioned his integrity: 'This man leads a double life': 'A break from Bond-age': 'This Colonel is not the owner of Follyfoot Farm but Q, the poker faced Major who kits out James Bond with all his lethal gadgets'.

By prior agreement with the producers of *Follyfoot*, Desmond flew to Las Vegas in May 1971 for one week to film his sixth Bond, *Diamonds Are Forever*. In this movie, Bond's search for the criminal hoarding quantities of black market diamonds, leads him from Holland to Las Vegas and ultimately to Ernst Stavro Blofeld, head of S.P.E.C.T.R.E. After the disastrous trail left by Lazenby, Cubby Broccoli and Harry Saltzman persuaded Sean Connery to return as 007 for the very last time. By all accounts, Sean capitulated simply because he was virtually given 'carte blanche' to name his own terms, conditions and salary.

Desmond welcomed his come back, but had mixed feelings about his first visit to Las Vegas, describing it as 'fascinating, frightening, exciting but flamboyantly revolting'. Nevertheless, he enjoyed his evening forays with director Guy Hamilton and other members of the cast to the casinos - but insists he left the gambling to them. "I am not a gambler of any sort unless, as in my *Diamonds* scene, winning is guaranteed." This scene shows Q with the pretty Jill St. John at the jackpot machines wearing a ring containing an electromagnetic rpm controller; a device that supposedly interferes with the machine's cylinders and ensures he wins.

With the sound of 10 cent pieces de-gorging themselves from the slots, Q fills his pockets and walks away. Off screen, he is quick to acknowledge, "This gadget is one of the few that definitely does not work, but the temptation of having all those 10 cent

The holster finger clamp. *Diamonds Are For Ever.*

pieces was too great and I fed every single one back into the machine - and didn't win a sausage." In direct contrast, the moon buggy, 007's lunar getaway vehicle in *Diamonds Are Forever* has today been groomed down and re-emerged as the dumpy quad bike used by farmers to scale difficult terrain.

Obviously, the producers felt the need to re-establish the gadgetry in this film after the almost total absence of it in *On Her Majesty's Secret Service*. There's a voice box resembling a telephone scrambler type contraption for changing and imitating voices. A holster finger clamp, looking distinctly like a mousetrap, lies in Bond's jacket pocket waiting for the enemy to frisk him; if they do, they'll find their fingers firmly encapsulated by the 'mousetrap's' steel teeth. There's a set of artificial skin fingerprints that peel on and off with ease. Finally, a piton gun that could shoot a steel peg with an attached rope into the side of the skyscrapers of Las Vegas, heralded the return of outlandish wizardry.

The awareness of just how prominent and popular the gadgets were to each film also extended to the man who always briefed Bond about them. Head of Publicity, Tom Carlile of UIP (United Independent Pictures), suddenly recognised the importance of Q and his representation of the mythical Q Branch. It was he who suggested to Saltzman that in order to publicize the forthcoming *Diamonds Are Forever*, Desmond should undertake a whistlestop tour of America in November, accompanied by the original battered briefcase featured in *From Russia With Love*, filled with gadgets; the twosome being chaperoned by Tom himself.

The trip proved something of an eye-opener for Desmond. "Tom was implicit in his instructions and told me it was essential to present the gadgets like an expert at interviews. I said to him, 'Look here, I'm an actor, I know nothing about gadgets. Until now I've just said my lines, collected the money and gone home'. 'Well, you'll damn well have to learn,' he replied. And learn I did, becoming quite an authority on the equipment supplied by Q Branch, although, I must admit, it was a bit nerve racking talking about it at first. Otherwise, I loved every minute of America. I loved all the attention. I loved the expression on the faces of the technicians at eight o'clock in the morning as I came on. You could tell they were thinking - 'what's this old fool doing?' - then the Bond music would begin and realisation dawned. I wish Pamela could have been with me, but Tom had one bad experience of taking somebody's wife on the publicity circuit and he said - never again."

The tour was a resounding success. Q was the darling of every American newspaper, they loved the quintessential boffin from England. At Fort Worth, a reporter quizzed him with: "I gather you get almost as much fan mail as Sean Connery?" To which Desmond dead-panned, "Yes, and this I'd like to credit to my devastating sex appeal. Unfortunately, a lot of it comes from schoolboys wanting to learn about explosives. One, who asked questions in great detail, I later discovered had plans to blow up his school." An amusing observation from another paper: 'Desmond Llewelyn walked past the hidden weapon detector at Philadelphia's International airport with a briefcase loaded with guns and the machine went berserk. But the security police who are there to grab hijackers just smiled. They had been warned Mr. Llewelyn, alias Q, was a very important man.' A half page article in the *Rocky Mountain News* illustrates just how well Desmond had slipped into his promotional role: 'The crusty Q talks smoothly about Connery, the beautiful girls, the tongue-in-cheek violence, the millions netted from Bond movies and, of course, the gadgets.' "Obviously you're something of an inventor yourself?" became a regular question. Sporting a wry grin, Desmond would reply, "Sorry to disappoint you, old chap, but I can barely change a light bulb, let alone repair the toaster. My wife says I'm utterly hopeless." As if to underline this fact, he then goes on to relate the story of a hotel lift which jammed with the door half open on the 25th floor. His lift companion obviously expected Bond's brilliant technical adviser to 'do something'. No such luck. With a touch of Bond humour, Q says he squeezed onto the fire escape, paused, unfazed and uttered, "What a damn fine view", then proceeded to climb the other fourteen flights to arrive, suitably winded, at his room.

To confirm the success of Desmond's first publicity tour, Tom Carlile emptied a file of press cuttings onto Harry Saltzman's desk. Saltzman, whom Desmond describes as a pocket Napoleon with a parched humour, glanced at them and muttered, "H'mm, you can wipe your arse with that lot."

As the flush of *Diamonds Are Forever* receded, Desmond and Pamela spent Christmas at their bolthole in Ireland, then went to Italy for ten days in February. There, Desmond, mildly puzzled by the vagaries of Turin's one-way system and fed up with the tram behind ringing its bell, turned left and inadvertently drove at speed down a walkway, oblivious of pedestrians skipping smartly out of reach. At the end, Pamela, who until now had been silent, turned and murmured, "I think you've just driven down the equivalent of The Burlington Arcade." However, his greatest moment of the holiday occurred in a deserted area in Pompeii, when a lone walker stared long and hard, then said in a broad Yorkshire accent, "Eh, lad, aren't you the Colonel in *Follyfoot*, can you give y'autograph, please?"

In early spring, filming resumed on the next thirteen episodes of *Follyfoot*, which was due to be televised during that summer - when its viewing would soar to an incredible twelve million. Desmond rented a little cottage at Sicklinghall for several months where he and Pamela explored the Yorkshire Dales in between shooting his scenes. In order to accommodate filming the next Bond, he'd been written out of *Follyfoot* for three episodes. This time, Roger Moore, his youthfully cherubic good

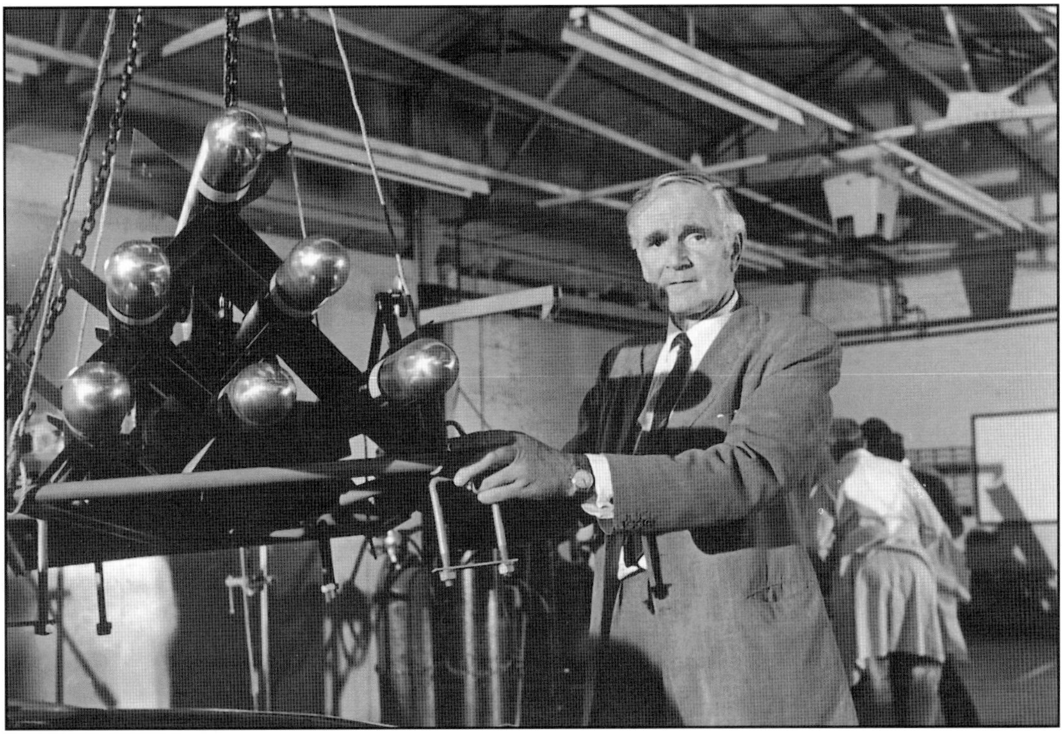

This photo was taken at the Aston Martin works whilst Desmond was filming *Diamonds Are For Ever*. Supposedly this was a part of Q's equipment for the next James Bond film. Unfortunately, he wasn't asked to appear in the production.

looks now blended into an aura of suave sophistication, had finally landed the role of 007 and Desmond was looking forward to working with him again. "Sean had been offered the earth to return, but he steadfastly refused. 'You've got to admire the bastard!' somebody remarked."

Live and Let Die turned out to be a bitter disappointment. After his personal euphoria over *Diamonds Are Forever*, Desmond was stunned when his agent phoned him with the bleak news: "Saltzman wants to do this one differently; he doesn't need you, after all." "I was so bloody fed up. Just when I seemed to be riding on a wave of certainty, the whole thing crashed down on me. Even to a bloody great tax bill dropping through the letter box."

Although *Live and Let Die* was devoid of Q in person, a few of his gadgets still came in useful. There's a magnetic Rolex watch, a special bug detector in Bond's toilet kit and a shark gun that fires high pressure capsules causing its target to blow up, but fans were suitably bereft when they discovered there was no Q to explain their intricate workings.

ALBERT R. BROCCOLI presents
ROGER MOORE
as IAN FLEMING'S
JAMES BOND 007
IN
"THE SPY WHO LOVED ME"
Directed by LEWIS GILBERT
United Artists
A Transamerica Company

- 8 -

NOW PAY ATTENTION 007

Q with 007 (Roger Moore) on *Moonraker*.

"Have you ever been told that you look just like Q,"
said the taxi driver.
"Well yes, it has been mentioned once or twice," I replied.

- 8 -
"NOW PAY ATTENTION 007."

As his sixtieth year approached, Desmond buried the disappointment of *Live and Let Die* together with the nagging worry of being pensioned out of Bond. He was prepared to believe the reasons for Q's non appearance were nothing personal, but a result of the growing unrest between Broccoli and Saltzman, the latter constantly needing the stimulation of different procedures.

Harry Saltzman bore all the hallmarks of a successful entrepreneur and gambler, yet like a heavy weight butterfly, his tubby frame housed a restless spirit requiring the excitement of ongoing challenges. Once the James Bond movies were up and running, he began to look elsewhere for new projects, new goals and new people. Inevitably, as his interest in adapting Fleming's Secret Agent 007 for the screen waned, so his relationship with Cubby faltered and their only common ground grew increasingly stony. The next Bond, *The Man with a Golden Gun* (1974) in which Q returns in person, would be their last.

Meanwhile, Desmond accepted a part in the TV play *Nine Tailors* in February 1974. This entailed playing a character who has a heart attack and dies: "Of which I'd had first hand experience, except for being dead." Happily alive after filming, he had time to chat to the leading man, Ian Carmichael, who reminded Desmond of their pre-war days when they appeared together in *R.U.R.* at the People's Palace in Mile End Road. An advertisement for a brand of tea, filmed at a glorious castle in the Midlands, stirred more 1930's memories when Desmond discovered his tea-time companion was the leading lady from The Forsyth Players, Mona Washbourne. A production of *Lloyd George Knew My Father* which eventually proved to be Desmond's penultimate stage appearance, was followed by television's *Man in the Zoo* and then *Love School*. "A marvellous play, all about pre-Raphaelite artists and such a lovely part, which made a change. Usually I'm given such tiny parts - just one day's work." Throughout, this constant and bewildered lament is hastily masked by his self-deprecating humour and honest charm as the smile returns: Desmond is not a man to dwell on misfortune.

With a sense of relief, it was back to Bond in August 1974, when Desmond worked with an old friend and new 007, Roger Moore, on *The Man with The Golden Gun*. Having cut his teeth on the previous film, Roger was now entrenched into walking, talking and thinking like James Bond and any lingering doubts as to his capabilities for exorcising Connery's ghost would disappear with his second appearance as the secret agent. The producers were delighted with their 'new man' and Desmond is full of praise for the way Roger achieved the difficult feat of breathing a different image into the accepted mould of 007. With hindsight, he thinks, "Of all the actors who have played Bond, Roger certainly had the hardest task. Obliterating an actor's inaugural portrayal of a character is always difficult; when it's somebody as sexy as Sean, it's twice as difficult and Roger knew the women would be sizing him up against his predecessor. Until Bond, Roger had been linked with his role as the clean cut, rather pretty boy in TV's *The Saint* with, so it is written, only two facial expressions; the first, lifting his left eyebrow for surprise and the second, the right eyebrow for fear. Maturity and sheer hard work on Roger's part altered all this and I think he played Bond, his Bond, to perfection. He was a bloody marvellous actor and I must say I had more fun working with him than any other. He had an enormous sense of humour and was a great practical joker, usually to my disadvantage."

Roger himself realised he couldn't emulate Connery's image of Bond and from the outset, he portrayed an altogether more humourously deliberate character, whose dress sense was even more immaculate. This reflected Roger's own impeccable style and measured personality. His middle class childhood, a good education, RADA and then National Service, gave him a methodical approach to his acting career and when he eventually landed the role of James Bond, he wasn't going to let it slip from his grasp. Subtly and skillfully he chiselled 007 to suit his own capabilities.

In spite of being directed by Guy Hamilton, responsible for blockbuster success of *Goldfinger, The Man with The Golden Gun* is not catalogued amongst the best Bond films. Desmond admits he can't remember anything about it, except that the suit he wore for filming is now in a private Bond Museum in America. "The guy who requested my suit for his museum was President of the Ian Fleming Foundation. At first, I said, no, I wear all my suits. Then, when I watched the film and later saw photographs of myself after a press conference, I realised how disreputable it looked!" Desmond's suits, or lack of them, have become legendary over the years, particularly when his favourite, crumpled, tweedy ensemble re-appeared yet again and elicited Roger's comment, "Oh my God, you're not wearing that old suit again?" But as Desmond points out, "It's alright for the 007's; their gear is provided: I have to wear my own clothes for Q's scenes."

The villain in *The Man with The Golden Gun*, is the notoriously accurate assassin, Scaramanga, played by Christopher Lee. His two outstanding trademarks are the ability to kill with one single bullet from his golden gun and the personal defect of having a third nipple. This leaves Q mildly embarrassed when he has to supply 007

Desmond and Roger Moore in their first Bond film together, *The Man With The Golden Gun*.

with a false nipple so as he can pose as Scaramanga. The nebulous plot, as far as Desmond can remember, has 'something to do with solar energy'. Even his own return, welcomed by all the Bond aficionados, was thin on the ground. So too were his gadgets: a Nikon camera which caused its subject to explode when aimed, a homing device and detector and not much else, apart from Q telling M he's 'working on a car that flies'. Thinking Q is being frivolous, M retaliates by replying, "Oh, do shut up Q." This, according to Desmond, is only the second time he has been called Q face to face on the screen. The first was in *Diamonds Are Forever* when Jill St. John gasps, "Oh, Mr. Q".

The production was not without mishaps and crazy tales, some of them more tense than others. One, showed the widening chasm between the two producers, when filming in Thailand had given Harry the idea of including an elephant chase. Cubby was in direct opposition, rightly assuming elephants would slow down the pace of an action-packed movie. Harry, however, had done some research and informed Cubby that the locals suggested elephants ran faster if they wore shoes! The outcome was sixty pairs of outsize shoes, a huge bill, a major row between the two producers and no elephant chase.

It was fairly clear to both concerned that the partnership required some drastic action. Cubby's ultimate interests lay with James Bond films, whilst Harry wanted to pursue other ventures. It was a battle of creative minds and formulas, neither wrong nor right, just different. Sadly, and after lengthy legal proceedings, the Saltzman/Broccoli partnership foundered and both went their separate ways; Cubby to continue with the 007 movies and Harry, having sold his shares in EON to United Artists, wherever fortunes beckoned.

The production of the BBC's *Anslem Gets a Chance*, offered a circumspective glance at a once considered future when Desmond played the vicar who will not allow his curate to preach. However, when the vicar falls ill, there is no alternative but to let him take his place and preach to the congregation. For a while, Desmond immersed himself happily in the character of a parson and afterwards, his son, Justin, remarked, "I always knew you were a sanctimonious old creep - you did it so beautifully."

Not quite so beautiful were the intense pains of angina that gripped Desmond while working on an episode of *The Onedin Line*. Somewhat shaken at their severity, he went to his doctor who handed him some pills, saying, "Take one of these whenever you feel a pain coming on, but do go carefully with them." A friend, who also happened to be a doctor, informed him otherwise, "Good Lord, the coxswain of the Brighton lifeboat takes those things like Smarties, nothing to worry about at all." With no ill effects, Desmond followed his friend's advice and for some years warded off the restrictive problems that accompany heart disease.

After tinkering with the script umpteen times, *The Spy Who Loved Me* (1977), resulted in a spectacular film with a plot woven around the wealthy shipping magnate, Karl Stromberg, whose main desire was to blow up the world and create his own underwater kingdom. Naturally, it's up to 007 to prevent him from annihilating the entire population, and to lend a helping hand is the stunning KGB agent, Major Anya Amasova, played by Barbara Bach. Together, they coast around Sardinia searching for a discreet entry into Stromberg's base, where they eventually discover bombs, sharks and Soviet and U.S. submarines, captured by a giant-sized, man-eating tanker that can open its bows and engulf unsuspecting subs.

For once, Desmond was in his element. Q had no less than four scenes and an arsenal of meaty gadgetry, much of it hidden in his Egyptian workshop disguised as a pyramid. In his first appearance in the film, he reels off long and impressive details on satellites, leaving his companions (and himself) looking utterly perplexed. Minutes

A surprise pouffe ejector seat at Q's workshop in Egypt. *The Spy Who Loved Me.*

The 'wet submersible' Lotus Esprit. *The Spy Who Loved Me.*

later, the cameras show him in his workshop placing a harmless looking tea tray on a long table. One quick turn of the hand and the tea tray skid-addles along the surface and lops off the head of his dining companion at the far end. "I want that ready for Akbar's tea party," quips Q.

The Spy Who Loved Me was the most ambitious Bond production yet. No expense was spared and Cubby, going it alone for the first time, wanted to make it the best. He even ordered Ken Adam, the production designer, to create the largest 007 sound stage in the world to shoot the massive sequences at Pinewood. Filming took place in extravagant locations; Egypt, the Bahamas, Scotland, Canada and Sardinia - where Desmond joined the cast in September 1976. "It came home to me just how much Cubby emulated the Bond standards in real life. The luxurious five-star hotel had been transformed, at Cubby's instigation, with six-star adornments. I had the most wonderful time."

He also found it thoroughly enjoyable when he helped the technicians paint the boats whilst waiting to film his third scene on Sardinia's sun-baked quayside. In the movie, a large container ship has anchored and Q's arrival is announced by the revving of an engine as he drives a Lotus Esprit, 007's new gadget bound car, on to the quay, where Bond, accompanied by Major Amasova, is awaiting its appearance. Having wished Major Amasova "Good morning", Q turns his attention back to Bond, uttering this much publicized phrase:

> "Now pay attention 007... I want you to take great care of this piece of equipment. There are one or two rather special accessories..."

His words are whipped away by a sudden breeze as 007, with his companion, climbs into the Lotus and accelerates away saying, "Q, have I ever let you down?"

This incredible Lotus, with extraordinary capabilities, including the ability to be driven underwater, was built by Oceangraphics in Florida. The logistics of this supposedly single piece of machinery took, say Lee Pfieffer and Phillip Lisa in their *Incredible World of 007*, 'Dozens of technicians at least three months of pre-planning and five weeks of filming for a scene that occupied less than three minutes of screen time.'

On screen, the imagination does a double take as 007 drives the Lotus off the edge of the quay straight into the sea after a hairy chase along Sardinia's coastline. At the press of a button, the wheels fold away to be replaced by fins, a rudder and a strengthened windscreen. In reality, four or five separate Lotus shells were required, apart from the normal land version. A basic body had to be used to negotiate the manoeuvres from land to sea, others simply depicted the external submarine features, with the retracting wheels and so on. Just one car had an engine and could actually travel underwater at a speed of around 7 knots. Technically speaking, this Lotus submarine is known as a 'wet submersible', meaning there is water inside and the pilot must wear breathing equipment. No wonder Q felt it needed 007's undivided attention. Nor did he have time to mention that his specially modified Lotus was fully equipped to fire underwater missiles and sea to air missiles. It also had a rear cement spray to eject onto a pursuing vehicle's windscreen, an oil release mechanism to cause skidding on land and provide a camouflage underwater. Quite a car, even by Q's standards.

Another rather endearing piece of equipment in *The Spy Who Loved Me* is 007's wet-bike, a kind of high-powered motorbike that can ride across water. Its inventor, Nelson Tyler, said wryly, "When I first thought of the idea in 1973, it worked like a dream - on paper. In practise, the thing sat immobile in the water with its engine purring like a kitten. At a loss to know what to do, I gave it a more powerful engine and it still sat there, this time roaring ferociously. Amendments to the rear ski finally

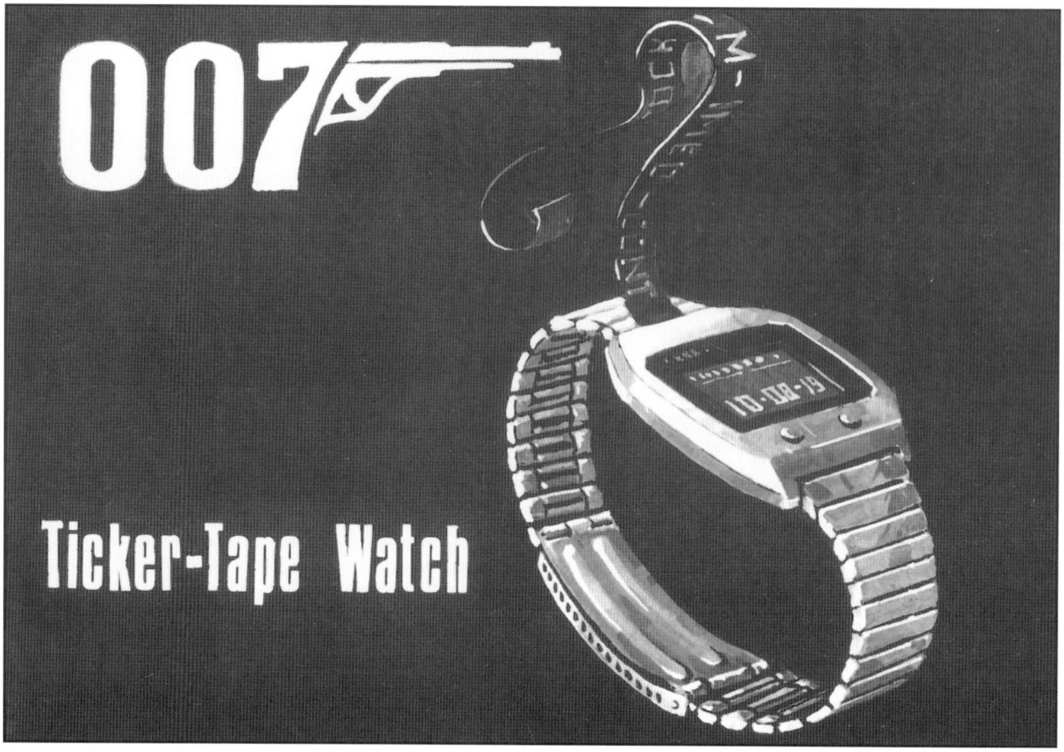

The Spy Who Loved Me.

got it cruising across the water, except when it turned, then everybody ended up in the drink. Eventually, adjustments to the front ski gave the bike the power to execute hairpin turns - and we were in business."

Yet another gadget, which in fact appears in the precursory shots of the film, is Bond's Seiko watch with a ticker tape read off. From this comes a message from M calling 007 back to London for an urgent assignment. Instantaneously, 007 extracts himself from the arms of a half naked woman and skis away from the snow-covered mountain retreat, culminating in the most spectacular ski chase before the titles have even hit the screen.

With his eighth Bond film completed and his fan mail increasing, Desmond felt he'd established Q as a 'legend within a legend'. Although the part was small, he enjoyed it thoroughly and had begun to benefit from related spin offs. He saw absolutely no reason why one should worry about getting typecast (particularly at his age), when he got such enormous pleasure and a reasonable amount of cash from a few days work.

Pamela, however, was not and never would be, keen on the Bond scenario. She disliked the brashness, the shallowness bored her and, according to her sons, she had even been known to nod off during the Premieres. Nor did she accompany Desmond when he went filming abroad - not even the delights of Sardinia's most exclusive hotel could lure her away from self-imposed responsibilities. "I'd have loved her to have been with me, but she always seemed to be looking after someone. Pamela gathered lame ducks like flies and, on this occasion her sister was unwell. I remember having to film an extra scene at Pinewood shortly after returning from Sardinia and saying to Pamela I'd get some manure from the farm on the way home. 'Hmm, collecting shit and shooting shit,' came back her rather unfair comment, but I think it summed up her attitude to Bond."

A diary for 1977 bears little resemblance to Q's gadget minded film persona, but it does indicate Desmond's increasing lack of other acting offers:-

> New Year: New Theatre, Hull (what the hell for). January: Voice on Bond. May 31st: Swan and Edgars, top floor, talking about Q. Got briefcase full of gadgets. Getting paid £50. Next Day: 'Come and meet Q' a complete flop. Nobody came. June: Did advert for Fiat, or was it Toyota, or both? June: 10.30 Upper Richmond Road. 7th July: Premiere of *The Spy Who Loved Me*. July: Hunstanton. Freezing cold. On location for *The Shrimp and the Anenome*, an L.P. Hartley trilogy. August: expenses £13.50, £18.50 and train at 4.30 pm. September: *Jim'll Fix It*. Boy wants to meet me and underwater car. Mustn't talk about guns - he's only a little boy. On the day: Jimmy Saville a charming blonde. October: filming at Brooklands. Lovely pre-war racing circuit. November: *Wilde Alliance* for Yorkshire TV. Small part, in Leeds University. November: Episode 8 included Julia Foster. Very nice. November: Rehearsal Kennington Oval.

The plain pages at the back of the diary are filled with Desmond's spidery handwriting, quite out of keeping with his large frame and generous nature. Almost unreadable, they call forth a backlog of horticultural memories. "Maybe it was the weather, or perhaps I'd obtained special fertilizer that year. We had quantities of vegetables - and soft fruit. I planted everything I could lay my hands on, cauliflowers, potatoes, carrots, leeks, globe artichokes, peas, tomatoes, runner beans, french beans, broad beans, mange-tout, spinach, even squash. Pamela said, 'We can't possibly eat all these. What the hell are you going to do with them?' The local greengrocer didn't want any more, said he was overloaded with stuff as it had been a good year for everybody. Not wanting to be stuck with a car load of veg, I did the rounds of all the other greengrocers and found one in Cooden who took the lot and gave me a better price. Fuelled by his promise of 'I'll take whatever you've got', I even tried to grow asparagus, with the help of our gardener, Ransome, who was a bit of a bugger - if he planted something, he automatically assumed half the yield was his."

'The man who gives James Bond the deadly touch,' wrote the *Evening Post* - one of half a dozen similarly headed reviews that continued to expound on the crusty boffin of Q Branch. Barely ten words were given over to *The Golden Lady*, the film that instigated the articles and had nothing whatsoever to do with Bond. In a roundabout way, reality was starting to dawn as Desmond conceded that the public only associated him with Q. The seed sown several years earlier, when almost every *Follyfoot* article billed him as Q, meant directors were disinclined to offer alternative characters, in spite of Desmond's: "If I wore a moustache or beard, nobody would recognise me." Changing agents to Roger Moore's, Denis Salinger, didn't help either. Curiously, the balance had imperceptibly altered from a career made up of numerous small roles with little recognition, to just a single, even smaller role, and world-wide fame.

Accepting that fate had juggled his life in a curious way, Desmond acknowledged he was more fortunate than most - he had the Bond safety net to rely on and the dearth of work in 1978, apart from a small amount of TV and radio, was atoned for by the freedom to have a long holiday in Ireland. The holiday helped Pamela get over the death of her father who, a year earlier, had been taken off all medication for general senility and other ills to enable him to pass away peacefully. Instead, he recovered and, except for his memory, lived for a further 11 months. In the odd moments of lucidity, his favourite comment was, "It's funny y'know, some people can remember the past and not the present, but I can't remember a damn thing."

Moonraker.

In September, Desmond started work on *Moonraker*. Shooting took place in the film studios in Paris and on location in Venice, South America and, so the pundits would have us believe, in outer space. The wildly impossible adventure is the least plausible of all the Bond escapades, but it reflected the current obsession with space age features. In this highly unlikely fantasy, 007 whizzes off into outer space as a part of his assignment from HQ, who have been ordered to sort out the disappearance of the U.S. space shuttle, Moonraker. Results are not long in coming as 007 tracks down the evil billionaire, Hugo Drax, whose personal wish is to create a space world inhabited by his own disciples, transported to their destination by the missing Moonraker. Not content with his space domain, Drax will then blast a series of satellites, containing a deadly nerve gas, earthwards and kill off the lesser mortals.

'Ludicrous, laughable but not dull', just one of many apt comments on *Moonraker*, released in 1979 to top all financial expectations - although, with hindsight, the makers agreed their excesses of 'sci-fi' didn't quite fit the Bond image. *Moonraker* is also the one film in which the gadgets from Q Branch are a little overshadowed by Drax's colossal space station. However, when 007 meets Q, carefully carrying a set of exploding bolas from his Brazilian workshop (disguised as a monastery), it produces an amusing exchange as 007 drily questions, "Balls, Q?" With an exasperated sigh Q replies, "Bolas, 007.", then proceeds to fling them at a waiting dummy, whose head flops forward as the bolas wind themselves round its neck and explode. "Well done, Q," observes 007, "must get those in the shops for Christmas!" Q's comprehensive list of gadgets is certainly the most extensive so far: a rather fetching sombrero clad, seated figure splits in half to reveal a machine gun; a cigarette case with X-ray apparatus for opening a safe; a Seiko watch with demolition apparatus and detonator; a high speed gondola (or Bondola) with hovercraft attributes; a laser gun;

The 'Bondola' in Venice. *Moonraker*.

a powered hang glider and a Q boat containing mine-laying capabilities and a homing torpedo.

Yet undoubtedly, Q's most unforgettable line of the entire film has nothing to do with gadgets. It occurs when he, M and other top brass are watching, on screen, the progress of the space capsule containing 007 and the lovely Dr. Holly Goodhead, hurtling home. As their embraces become intimate and the signals fuzzy, M demands to know what Bond is doing whilst Q, peering askance at the screen, suggests "I think he's attempting re-entry...!"

Desmond has poignant memories of filming *Moonraker* in Paris with Bernard Lee (M). Unbeknown to either, Bernard was in the early stages of cancer and this would be his final Bond. Although he was taken to the set of the subsequent production, *For Your Eyes Only*, he was too ill to participate and died a few months later in 1981. As a mark of respect Cubby refused to have anybody else play his part in this movie and the script was re-written so that M was referred to only in name. There was enormous sadness at his death and Desmond, in particular, grieved at the passing of an erstwhile friend and great eccentric.

"Bernie was such a lovely man, a flawless actor, a delightful drunk and, yes, undoubtedly one of the last great eccentrics. On one occasion, we were at some hotel in Paris (Pamela came with me when I did *Moonraker*) having dinner, when Bernard suddenly spotted a piano. Immediately, he wandered over and started playing the thing. He didn't ask anybody's permission, nor did he worry about the other diners. He just went on playing until, eventually, we left him there, still playing and quite oblivious to everybody else; but that was Bernard for you. I remember another time going into a casino with him and seeing Cubby at one of the tables. 'Hi there. You two going to play?' he asked. 'Not for me, Cubby,' I said, getting

Desmond and Pamela at the premiere of *Moonraker*.

in before Bernie. 'Ah, g'wan, have these and enjoy yourselves.' And as he turned his back to concentrate on the game a wad of notes landed at our feet. After that, Bernie was impossible. He ambled from table to table hoping to chance upon a winning streak. By the end of the evening, he was happily broke and I still clutched an only slightly depleted wad of fivers."

Until the next James Bond got under way, Desmond can recall little about his checkered appearances or the increasing amount of garden fetes he was asked to open. The TV series *Hazell* only left an impression of watching Concorde fly overhead. *Speed King*, a film about Malcolm Campbell, made him think, 'What a 'so and so' the man must have been.' A couple of weeks in Cheltenham filming *The Happy Autumn Fields*; a week at the Cardiff TV studios for *The Life of Lloyd George*, are blanks. However, a spell at Wapping for the making of *Dr Jekyll and Mr. Hyde* returned him to the scene of his boyhood and evoked memories of occasionally staying at the Radley Mission during school holidays. He remembers the excitement of riding on the back of Father Lean's motorbike when he visited patients at the hospital in Mile End Road or the 'less fortunate' who hung around the West End. The spicy smell, like a mix of oranges and cinnamon, exuded from the old warehouses around Wapping, which to Desmond's chagrin, "have all gone now. Bombed, I suppose, during the war, but at least St. Peter's Church was left intact." His musings, which move on to a disastrous play in Hayes with Nicholas Parsons, were not quite so pleasant. It brought Desmond on stage for the very last time where he had a complete block and, to his horror, forgot all his lines.

As 1980 rolled to a close, so the filming of Bond No. 12 began. Enter John Glen, who had previously been involved with *On Her Majesty's Secret Service, The Spy Who Loved Me* and *Moonraker* as second unit director and editor. His expertise in action sequences was famed, both in film and television, yet it's suggested he was marginally apprehensive when Cubby finally handed him the leading reins of *For Your Eyes Only*. It resulted in a fascinating screen thriller and John, his talent proven, went on to direct four successive Bond movies. With John came a wicked sense of humour that almost matched Roger's and Desmond commonly became the butt of their practical jokes. "I was sitting in the corner of the set, rehearsing my part, when John came over and said, 'Look I'd like you to learn these extra lines for this afternoon's shooting', and handed me a sheet of paper covered in technical gobbledygook. 'I can't possibly learn this in time,' I replied aghast. Whereupon, John muttered, 'of course, you can' and pushed off. Two hours later, he returned with Roger, both grinning broadly. 'Don't worry Q,' they chorused, 'we've decided not to use those lines after all.' Rotten sods, I'd missed lunch, too, but they were always in cahoots together. One of Roger's favourite tricks was to stick a notice across my 'idiot' boards saying 'Bollocks Q'. Another time, he, and John again, managed to convince me I was going to have to play Q's scene in a minuscule pair of shorts. Heedless of my protests, they handed me this ridiculous piece of clothing, then fell about laughing."

In fact, Desmond did have one very complicated scene with Roger in *For Your Eyes Only*. Here, Q's jargon is technically convoluted and Desmond had enormous difficulty pronouncing words he'd never heard of before. What made things doubly difficult was having to simultaneously operate a computer - when he'd never used one in his life. Time and again, the scene went wrong until Roger suggested that as 007 was an authority on computers, he should operate it instead. Having agreed the alteration, a computer expert stepped forward to explain the procedure to Roger, who, Desmond reckoned, "did the whole thing a damn sight better than the professional. Roger was brilliant. Not only could he reel off his lines without faltering, but mine too."

For Your Eyes Only returned to the more basic espionage thrills that *Moonraker* lacked, but the ingredients, so essential to any Bond, remained: the terrifying action

Q wears his Greek priest's gear. *For Your Eyes Only.*

sequences, the miscreants and the stunning women were once more combined to test the strength of James Bond. Q doesn't have as many gadgets, apart from a special climbing rope (used by 007 to shin up the face of a mountain fortress), a binocular camera and a Seiko watch that can transmit messages. The Lotus Esprit re-enters this film with one or two necessary modifications from Q branch. Q himself, makes an amusing appearance in Greece, disguised as a priest, and when 007 nips into the confessional, saying, "Forgive me Father, I have sinned," he gleefully answers, "That's putting it mildly 007."

In June 1981, after the film's Premiere, which was attended by both Prince Charles and Lady Diana, Desmond asked Roger if he was going to do the next Bond film. Before Roger had time to reply, his daughter chipped in and said, "Oh Daddy, you can't possibly be in the next Bond, you're much too old!"

- 9 -

A CONTINUING PHENOMENON

Q's Indian Rope trick. *Octopussy*.

"The public don't want Bond to change.
They prefer the fantasy,
escapism and larger-than-life elements."

- 9 -
A CONTINUING PHENOMENON

"After all this time you'd have thought people would have got fed up with the James Bond movies, but no; the magic still grips them and, if anything, they've soared to a greater zenith. I think the credit lies with Cubby who always followed Hitchcock's advice, 'you need climax after climax to ensure success.' His golden rule paid off handsomely."

Apart from Bond and a number of radio broadcasts, plus the wedding of his younger son, Justin, to Sarah, the first two years of the eighties were remarkably uneventful. The thirteenth 007 movie significantly changed things.

"I made my first real money from *Octopussy* and had three or four decent scenes instead of a momentary appearance". Ignoring his daughter's comment about age, Roger returned as 007 and gave one of his best performances. John Glen, once again in the director's hot seat, incorporates mind-bending stunt work and action throughout and his ability to harvest the last drop of talent from cast and crew alike, is plainly apparent. Aesthetically, the colourful backdrop of India makes the film probably the most pleasing of the series and it remains one of Desmond's favourites.

The principal setting is Udaipur in India, where the lakeside scenery is a colourful mix of tiny islands and marble palaces. At least half of the local population are garbed in brilliant saris and jostle side by side with oxen and motorised rickshaws through the streets, gardens and bazaars of Udaipur. On the mountainous ridge behind lies a magnificent, if formidable, palace that once belonged to the rulers of Udaipur. It was against this hot, dusty, bustling background that the filming of *Octopussy* began in 1982.

The spectacular pre-title aerial sequence of the movie features the appealing Acrostar mini jet; the only model of the world's smallest jet plane belonging to Corkey Fornoff, of Louisiana, USA. Capable of a top speed of 310 mph and a ceiling of 30,000 feet, this amazing little mini jet was invented, manufactured and flown in the film by Corkey, a highly skilled stunt pilot. The compact dimensions of this incredible aircraft, which is powered by a single jet engine are: 12 foot in length, 5 foot 8 inches in height and a wing span of 17 foot. In the film, these wings are shown as retractable, enabling the jet to be hidden behind the rear end of a false horse in a trailer to provide an instant getaway for Bond.

Slightly less spectacular, but definitely more bizarre, are the opening shots of *Octopussy* presenting a garishly costumed clown pursued by a couple of knife throwers. As the clown climbs a high-wire fence, a knife lands in his back and he falls, spread-eagled, into fast flowing water. Still with the knife in his back, he clambers up an embankment further downstream, staggers amongst undergrowth before crashing through French windows and dropping outstretched and, not surprisingly, dead on the carpet of a glossy residence. In his hand, he clasps the priceless Faberge Egg, the jewel encrusted linchpin of the film.

The title character of 'Octopussy' is played by Maud Adams, a brittle beauty with her own entourage of similarly endowed acrobatic female assistants. Octopussy runs a shady, but successful, circus created from the profits of her main interest, jewellery smuggling. Her partner in crime, and 007's unctuous chief adversary, Kamal Khan (Louis Jordan) is anxious to get hold of the Faberge Egg and when it comes up for

Watched by 007 and Vijay (Bond's Indian ally), Q plants the homing device in the Faberge Egg. *Octopussy*.

auction at Sotheby's, he's there to bid. So is Bond, and as the price escalates, Khan is forced to pay half a million, unaware he's bid for a fake. The plot thickens as Kamal Khan returns to India and 007 follows, only to find himself plunged into a Cold War conspiracy, murder and intrigue... and Octopussy.

To be on hand for 007, Q grudgingly trudges out to India to set up his workshop, cunningly constructed behind a billboard in one of Udaipur's maze of alleys. Having just been involved in a whacky street chase, 007 pops in to see Q, looking slightly dishevelled and his, "How are you Q," gets a testy reply. "Most unhappy, 007, thanks to you. There are no proper facilities here. So how can I possibly be expected to retain the quality of my work...?" The familiar tones disguise the practised irritation that has become the backbone of every Bond production; the very briefest of Q's scenes arouse a quintessential humour leaving an underlying curiosity about the actor with so little screen time. However, in *Octopussy*, the fans are treated to a little more of his crusty discourse as 007 follows him through the workshop where a rigid rope (referred to as Q's Indian Rope Trick) spirals towards heaven. Suddenly, it flops at right angles. "Having problems in keeping it up Q?", enquires 007. "An experimental model," snaps Q. Together, they watch the testing of a lethal spiked door apparatus before getting down to the business of the Faberge Egg, the most important prop in *Octopussy* and an exact replica of the priceless Coronation Egg.

Originally by Carl Faberge, the egg was presented to Her Imperial Highness, The Tzarina Fedoronova by His Imperial Highness The Tzar Nicholas II in the year 1897. This intricate work of art, fashioned in filigree gold and enamel set with diamonds, sapphires, pearls and rubies, opened to reveal a minute gold and enamel coach.

Looking vulnerable in Q's distinctively large hands ("a bonus as nobody can dub them"), he hides a homing device and microphone within the replica egg, gives it to Bond, then turns his attention to a fountain pen lying alongside.

> Q: "This pen releases a nitric acid mixture capable of dissolving all metals."
>
> 007: "Wonderful for poison pen letters."
>
> Q: "Oh, do pay attention 007. Now if you pull the top of the pen there's a sensitive hearing device that acts as a receiver for the egg..."

The conversation continued intermittently as Bond wandered around the workshop fiddling with the gadgets. The pained look from Q obviously expressed aggravation and his patience (what little he had) gave way.

> Q: "Really, 007, I haven't time for such adolescent antics. Do get along, I've got my work to do."

The timing is perfect, the interchange amusing, the 'old boy' persona, refreshingly out of place in the world of 007, the appearance too short; Q's fans want more. But the film makers are clever and the pithy scenes leave Q, the reaper of brilliant gadgetry, as a lovable mystery.

His next appearance in *Octopussy* is by the lakeside at Udaipur. It's dusk and Q is sitting fishing whilst waiting for 007 who is investigating Octopussy's floating palace. When his 'next- on-watch' asks if there's any sign of Bond, he responds rather crossly: "You must be joking. If 007's on an island entirely populated by women, we won't see him till dawn." And with that parting shot he stomps off into the tropical Indian darkness. Except it wasn't. Much to Desmond's disappointment, Q had been fishing in a man-made pond in Pinewood studios. "And I'd so hoped for a few days in India."

Even in his final scene, where he pilots a hot air balloon, complete with closed circuit TV cameras and receiver screen, he only rose a few feet off the ground - but as he says, "At least it got me out of the workshop."

Nevertheless, 007 is doubtful of his chief equipment officer's airborne capabilities. "Can you handle this contraption Q?" he enquires. With a withering glance, Q responds, "It goes by hot air." "Oh, in that case you can," replies 007, lifting the famous Moore eyebrow.

After the balloon has made a bumpy landing on Octopussy's floating palace, Bond sprints off, leaving his pilot to be mercilessly fondled by Octopussy's ladies. Demonstrating an engaging gruffness, Q waves a hand indifferently saying, "Oh never mind that now... well, later perhaps."

Desmond recollects the scene being done a few days before Christmas. "The studios were freezing: the girls were covered in goose pimples and Roger was fed up with shooting the same thing again and again. The poor chap wanted to fly home to Switzerland for the holiday."

Amid a fountain of press and TV coverage, the Premiere of *Octopussy* took place on 6th June 1983, once again in the presence of Prince Charles and Princess Diana. Even more exciting was the pre-launch promotional tour of America which Desmond had undertaken with two of Octopussy's girls, Mary Stavin and Janine Andrews. It was the first time he'd been on the publicity circuit for Bond since *Diamonds Are Forever* in 1971, and he loved it.

The press followed him everywhere, faithfully recording every comment. On the 5th June the *Sunday Herald News* quoted:-

The hot air balloon lands on Octopussy's floating palace.

> 'I had four entrances in the script and frankly I thought I'd be OK for a months work. I'm paid on a time basis, you see. But I hadn't counted on the director, John Glen, who was so damned efficient I'd finished in a few days.'

Another reported, '*Octopussy's* relatively short on gadgets, but long on Llewelyn and he's a delight.'

The *Toronto Star* of 27th May, asked Desmond if the role of Q had typecast him to such an extent that it had ruined his acting career. Disarmingly, he responded, "I'm 69 and no longer ambitious. After all, if it hadn't been for Q, maybe I wouldn't have had a career at all, nor would I be surrounded by these lovely Bond Ladies." Accordingly, Mary and Janine smile and drape themselves against his shoulder as he manages to be both avuncular and charming with them.

Other headlines followed: 'Butterfingers Q is the Wizard of Bond'; 'Gardens not gadgets for Q; 'Gadgets master gets a piece of the action'; 'An explosive situation as 007's Q hits the town,' wrote the *New York Post* on 31st May. They then enlightened their readers:-

> 'The tall stranger known to most people as Q came through Kennedy Airport Customs with several pistols and daggers, a fountain pen that spurts acid, a package clearly marked 'Explosives' and a letter saying, in effect, he was harmless.'

Interestingly, Desmond did actually carry a letter from EON Productions on his *Octopussy* travels. Headed 'To whom it may concern', it read:-

> 'Mr. Desmond Llewelyn is the actor who plays Q in the James Bond films. He is travelling to the United States to promote *Octopussy* prior to its release in June. In this connection, he will be carrying a number of

theatrical props from all the Bond films, which will be returned to the UK with him. They include: a replica piton gun: a replica Walter PPK: 2 stage daggers: 1 tin talc: a finger trap: an underwater camera: spector ring: model car: model Moonraker: 1 bleeper.'

Alongside, EON had written 'of no commercial value'. Little did they realise that within a few years every piece of Bond memorabilia would be avidly sought after by enthusiastic collectors willing to pay hundreds or even thousands of pounds for the most minor piece of equipment.

Back in New Orleans, one interviewer took a perverse pleasure in describing Desmond's lack of mechanical skills:-

'Here to promote *Octopussy*, Llewelyn carried several of the props used in past 007 movies, including the original attache case. This required the combined efforts of both the actor and the writer of this article to open: during the struggle, Llewelyn's glasses fell off and broke. He then tried to position a mock knife in a spring loaded ejection device inside the case, only to have the weapon flop onto the carpet. Later, Llewelyn produced the actual wristwatch television set introduced by Seiko for the new film. He mentioned that a publicist in another town had got a picture, but he couldn't make it work at all.'

The same reporter also interrogated Desmond closely on the rival production, *Never Say Never Again*; a remake of *Thunderball* produced by Broccoli's old adversary, Kevin McClory, and inexplicably starring a lean, tanned Sean Connery as 007, but, interestingly, no Q. Desmond neatly side-stepped his questions by observing, "Thank God, I wasn't asked to play in this movie. I'm not under contract to Cubby, but it's thanks to him I've had the chance to tour the world. He's remarkable y'know and as a producer, he still obeys all Fleming's rules, even though he's run out of books."

Most approached the Gadget Master more kindly; one, quaintly referring to him as 'Guinness sipping Sprite'. Another, 'Desmond Llewelyn is the picture of a distinguished English gentleman, his silver hair sets off a well-dressed appearance topped off by a navy blue tie adorned with a small 007!' Amusingly, Desmond draws attention to the gold fountain pen from *Octopussy*. "If the pen contains a reservoir of lethal acids capable of melting any metal, why the hell," he asks, "doesn't it melt the pen?" Although he enjoyed his 'inability to handle gadgets' approach, he excelled on TV's *Blue Peter* when he appeared with the Acrostar minijet and explained all its gadgets with the aplomb of an expert.

Undoubtedly, the most outstanding occurrence during Desmond's *Octopussy* travels happened in this country when he visited Plymouth for a charity premiere. Here, he came face to face with the real life Q, Charles Fraser-Smith - the man thought by many to be Ian Fleming's inspiration for Q Branch.

After a number of years as an agricultural missionary in Morocco, Charles Fraser -Smith returned to London in 1940. Anxious to contribute in some way to the war, he jumped at the chance of a job with the Ministry of Supply in Leeds. His post of Civil Servant appeared shrouded in secrecy, particularly as the headquarters of MI6 were adjacent to the MoS headquarters in London. After a few weeks in Leeds, Charles was informed he was being moved to the London HQ, but first, and without too much explanation, he must sign the Official Secrets Act.

Throughout the war, Charles and his assignments were clothed in the anonymity of an ordinary Civil Servant. In reality, he masterminded much of the equipment used by our spies, resistance workers and prisoners of war planning to escape. Hollowed out golf balls for messages: shaving brushes concealing maps: shoe laces with a razor sharp edge: fountain pens with secret cavities: a darning mushroom used to land light aircraft, were just a few of Charles's gadgets. By Bond standards, this equipment seems dull and unimaginative. In the 1940's, it was vital and a brilliant adjunct to winning the war. Some 40 years later, when the period of official secrecy expired, Charles wrote of his 1940 - 1945 experiences in *The Secret War of Charles Fraser-Smith*. He was later fascinatingly portrayed by the biographer, David Porter, in *The Man Who Was Q - The life of Charles Fraser-Smith.*

Charles first became acquainted with Ian Fleming during the war when the latter, having studied Fraser-Smith's work, supposedly requested some secret equipment for the Naval Intelligence. Whether this is true or not, is debatable, but it is recognised that both men incurred favourable impressions of the other from that meeting. Just how much of Fraser-Smith's wartime profession influenced Fleming's writings is also debatable. Yet even the smallest seed of wizardry Fleming planted in his Bond thrillers, was even more successfully cultivated and presented for the films by screenwriter, Richard Maibaum who, in essence, should have the credit for creating Q.

Desmond found Charles a fascinating man and a very religious one, too. "For some reason, he gave me a copy of the Lord's Prayer written in a Devon 'accent'. He thought the James Bond movies were great fun, but disliked the sex scenes. When we made a television programme together at the Plymouth studios, many viewers remarked on our uncanny facial resemblance and, apparently, he was often referred to as 'Q The Original', sometimes signing himself thus. When he died, a lot of people thought it was me and Pamela kept getting these phone calls of condolence. A couple of newspapers positively stated I was dead and got a bit of a shock when I phoned them up saying: 'This is a voice from the other side...!'" In March 1993, after the death of Charles Fraser-Smith, Desmond opened an exhibition of all his gadgets, together with some from Q Branch, at Dover Castle.

Having flitted around England for various *Octopussy* premieres, Desmond, accompanied by Pamela, continued his publicity tours. He admits to thoroughly enjoying all the travelling and the attention. An added bonus was being extremely well paid; even Pamela sagely remarked: "At long last Bond is beginning to pay off." As usual Desmond captured his globe trotting activities with his hap-hazardous scribble in a diary:-

> July: Stockholm, wonderful time. Went round a castle with a theatre inside. Flew from Stockholm to Hamburg. Lots of luggage. Bond briefcase with gadgets lost - finally discovered it had been taken away for safety. Went to Berlin. Saw wall. Taxi driver not German, but very anti-British. On to Munich. Weather very hot. No air conditioning in hotel. Sat in beer keller instead.
>
> August: Ireland for two weeks holiday. Toronto for three days. A Toyota ad. - got £1000 for the job.
>
> September: Flew to Luxembourg. This time carried briefcase through customs after telling the man there were guns in it. All OK, but Pamela searched thoroughly! Toured Luxembourg. Interviewed by a French woman for TV, but couldn't hear what the interpreter said. On to Paris. Pamela incensed because somebody pointed to me and said, 'Look there's M.' Used the Metro as it's cheaper than taxis. Looked in on Maxim's.
>
> October: Booked a trip to visit friends in America. Phone rang. EON asking me to promote *Octopussy* in Australia? Said no. Ordered APEX tickets and going to America with Pamela instead. Phone rang again.

Publicity travels on behalf of *Octopussy*. From left to right:- Janine King, John Glen (director), Pamela and Desmond, in Singapore.

> How about going to Australia via America, First Class and all found? Said yes, immediately. Stayed on an island off Maine. Visited our friends. Saw the Mayflower. Sadly, didn't eat lobster. V. disappointed in 'the Fall' - just trees after bloody trees. Went to Los Angeles.
>
> November: Australia. Landed in Brisbane. John Glen on publicity tour as well. Flew to Sydney. Beautiful. Robert Helpmann there. Flew back to Brisbane. Gold Coast lovely. Lunched at Ryans. Pamela said lavatory pretty basic but after being shown the 'great outdoors', where people were picnicking, it was preferable. Drove down Duck Bill Road, very wild, got lost briefly. On to Melbourne. Stayed at Regent Hotel. Back to Sydney. Bond publicity party on boat. Given a Mont Blanc pen. John got a girlfriend with him. Auckland for the day. Adelaide - an orderly city. Perth for five days. Singapore for weekend. Lots of publicity with John. Fabulous revolving restaurant. 24th November: Home.

During the countless interviews, Desmond quickly became accustomed to parrying questions. One that frequently occurred was, 'What about the gorgeous Bond women? Does your wife get jealous?' To which he produced a standard reply. "No, she doesn't get jealous, because I never really meet them. To date, I have only worked with the Bond girls once and that's on the current film *Octopussy*. Oh, I did have some scintillating dialogue with Barbara Bach in *The Spy Who Loved Me*, when I say 'Good morning, Major Amasova'. I had a few words with Jill St John in *Diamonds Are Forever* and I waved to Diana Rigg in *On Her Majesty's Secret Service*. So, disappointing as it may be for everybody, I'm afraid the Bond ladies are not one of my fringe benefits."

All in the line of duty. Q, Miss Moneypenny, 007 and M at Ascot. ***A View To A Kill.***

In August 1984, Desmond began filming *A View To A Kill*. Financially, he felt a little more complacent and when asked, 'What had all the money he'd earned from Q done for him?' replied, "At least I know that when the wind blows and all the tiles fall off the roof, I can afford to have them put back again." He did go on to admit that Q had unquestionably been responsible for lessening his acting horizons and in the last eight months he'd only done one advert for Phillips radio (as Q), a couple of TV interviews (on Q) and a few radio broadcasts (about Q). In between times, he'd continued the ongoing task of shoring up Linkwell, had a hernia operation, bought a corgi puppy and christened him Hyphen-Jones, "on account of the Welsh aristocracy always calling themselves Something-Jones."

Recognition as Q often bordered on the absurd and Desmond recalled the situation when he handed Pamela's watch to a disinterested jeweller for repair. The jeweller's bored expression suddenly flickered into life when he acknowledged his customer. 'I've seen you before. You're er..., you're in those Bond things - making all the gadgets. Got it... you're Q. But surely you could mend your wife's watch? No... come on, you must be kidding.' "People," says Desmond flatly, "simply do not seem to understand I'm an actor and in real life most gadgets expire or explode as soon as I touch them."

A View To A Kill emulated the *Goldfinger* type of fantasy, except gold bullion and Fort Knox were replaced by microchips and Silicon Valley. Desmond remembers little about the production except spending some days top-hatted at Ascot with 007, M and Miss Moneypenny; all in the line of duty, of course. Off screen, Cubby commented on Desmond's unusually pristine morning suit only to be told, "It had been bequeathed by a dear friend after we'd visited him in hospital and Pamela had complained how dreadfully scruffy I looked in mine. From the depth of the bedclothes, a surprisingly

Cubby Broccoli.

cheerful voice said, 'I'm not for this world much longer, I'll leave you mine with pleasure!' And he did."

The savage fire that razed the 007 set to the ground at Pinewood studios just before shooting *A View To A Kill*, could have been seen as an ill-omen. Certainly, the film was not without its problems and personality clashes. Accepting these hazards were a part of the film industry as well as being accustomed to making quick decisions, Cubby ordered the set rebuilt. Within four months it had been completed and shooting began slightly ahead of schedule.

Grace Jones, the leading villainess 'May Day', was an altogether different problem. Her lean, dusky and bizarre appearance reminded one of an unpredictable lioness about to pounce. "She was an absolute menace and I believe she gave Cubby's daughter, Barbara, (she looked after Grace) a hell of a time with all her outrageous demands."

Regrettably, but understandably, *A View To A Kill* provided the swan song for two favourites, 007's Roger Moore and Lois Maxwell, who had portrayed Miss Moneypenny since the inaugural *Dr. No*. Anno Domini had begun to make a marked presence and to have an ageing Miss Moneypenny making eyes at an ageing 007, didn't quite fit the Bond image. It was time for change. "She made a wonderful Miss Moneypenny and always played her hidden passion, visible in the underlying sexual repartee scenes with 007, to absolute perfection. Ian Fleming once told Lois 'You are exactly the Miss Moneypenny I envisaged, tall and elegant with the most kissable lips in the world'. She loved that. I was very sad to see Roger go, but being Roger, he left like a gentleman, with a handshake and the acknowledgement that it had been a good run. He, too, was aware that make-up could no longer disguise the insidious wrinkles, in spite of physically being in good shape. There's no doubt the light humourous touch he gave James Bond won him international acclaim."

Snooper, the robot surveillance machine in *A View To A Kill*.

The role of Q, remained unaffected by wrinkles and the ageless paternalism he sometimes bestowed on Bond made one believe he could be immortal. Sadly, he's not much in evidence in this film and suggests his 'piece de resistance' scene, due to be shot in San Francisco, was axed - "by some bloody hatchet man." Nor are his gadgets particularly spectacular: a camera/ring with a lens in the centre jewel; a bug detecting and listening device under the head of a razor; a modified credit card for breaking and entering through windows; special polarised sun glasses; a device able to pick up previously written material from the indentation marks and, last but not least, Snooper, a small robot surveillance machine.

This pop-eyed contraption gives the appearance of a motorised cat and does Q who is conducting a screen search for 007, no credit at all. When Snooper discovers Bond in the shower with the attractively soapy Stacey (Tanya Roberts), he sits there ogling like a pint-sized Peeping Tom and Q is forced, via Snooper, to relay to HQ that "007 is just cleaning up a few details!"

In the summer of 1985, Desmond began his publicity travels for *A View To A Kill* with the British actress Fiona Fullerton (Soviet KGB agent Pola Ivanova) across South America. In Rio, Desmond met Ronnie Biggs whom he describes with obvious disappointment as rather a pathetic man; otherwise he and Fiona were richly feted across the entire continent and had "a fantastic time". Pamela was unable to accompany Desmond as she'd had an operation prior to the trip and been forced to remain in England to recuperate. "Fiona was an absolute sweetie and extremely attractive. And yes - if circumstances had been different and I'd muscled up enough courage, I might have made some tentative approaches, although I'm pretty certain she'd have told me to 'bugger off'. But as I've said before, I just adored Pamela and that stopped me from straying - even when I wanted to."

Publicity in South America with Fiona Fullerton. *A View To A Kill*.

"When I kept forgetting my lines, the director told me to keep the mask on and he'd dub them afterwards." *The Living Daylights.*

Describing it as 'a string of little things', Desmond was kept occupied on and off until another Bond got under way. Whilst not of the acting nature, it was nevertheless gratifying and financially rewarding to be in demand for advertisements, judging competitions and promoting computer games, as well as the inevitable products and programmes tied in with Q and his gadgets.

Meanwhile, the crucial search hotted up for the new James Bond and, according to Desmond, every actor he subsequently met claimed to have auditioned for the role. The popular choice lay with the thirty-five year old Pierce Brosnan, who was all but signed up for the part when TV executives refused to waive his contract on the television series, *Remington Steele*. Cubby's finger had to point elsewhere and it quickly crooked on the long-considered Timothy Dalton. Desmond confirms that, "Timothy was an entirely different kettle of fish to Roger or Sean. As a trained classical actor, his approach to portraying James Bond was totally individual and some say it was the nearest to Fleming's Bond. Being a stage actor, he delved deeply into the character and made no concessions. If 007 had been in a fight, Timothy insisted he should have the hallmarks of a fight; his hair would be matted, his clothes dishevelled and there would be blood on his chin. Quite unlike Roger, who simply had to straighten his tie afterwards."

Timothy Dalton's debut as 007 in *The Living Daylights* (1987), called forth mixed comments. Having been used to suspense laced with humour, the critics were uncertain if they liked his interpretation of James Bond as a seriously dangerous secret agent. Gone were the gags of the Moore era, and those throwaway one-liners, so good from Connery, somehow fell uncomfortably from Dalton's lips.

"Although my scenes at Pinewood studios were over in less than a week, I personally found Timothy the easiest and most professional Bond to work with. But he was adamant that his 007 would be made of steely stuff and not a chocolate box hero."

In this film Q's gadgets are more outlandish and a brand new Aston Martin Volante is introduced as 007's swish vehicle. Duly tinkered with by Q Branch, the Aston Martin has a few useful, personalised accessories: a windscreen with a head-up visual display; a scanning digital radio; bullet proof glass; a fireproof body; guided missiles concealed behind the lights; a jet engine booster rocket; weapons control panel; convertible ice tyres; retractable snow skis hidden in the door sills; a laser cutting device in the wheel hubs and a self destruct mechanism - applied in a most impressive escape sequence. Justifiably, Q is pleased with these little extras and appears in a good mood when he demonstrates a portable radio cassette which turns into a mini rocket. To 007, he jokes, "Something we're making for the Americans - it's called a Ghetto Blaster." He also exhibits a couch that literally swallows its comfortably seated victim.

From Q Branch, Bond has a cache of wearable equipment: a key ring that emits 'stun gas' together with a key ring finder packed with highly concentrated explosives. One is activated by a wolf whistle; the other by whistling *Rule Britannia*. Finally there's a pen that duplicates what another pen writes by means of a radio receiver.

Did the public find Dalton's Bond overly authentic or was it too early to tell? The plot, whereby 007 is assigned to arrange the defection of the top Soviet general, had been scripted for an unknown Bond and therefore Timothy had little room for manoeuvre. Maybe it was the sheer curiosity of a new 007 which led to the Box Office grossing more on *The Living Daylights* than the previous *A View To A Kill*. Whatever, Desmond is unyielding in his praise for both the film and its star. "Timothy comes across as his own man and neither tried nor wanted to emulate Sean Connery or Roger Moore. To get the hype aroused, the pre-launch publicity was enormous. I remember being involved in the one hour television programme *Happy Anniversary 007*, ostensibly celebrating 25 years of the James Bond movies; in reality it gave Timothy a huge plug. There was also a live radio programme on Bond which was broadcast in the early morning, so I stayed with Ivor in London the night before. Unfortunately, come dawn, the damn car wouldn't start and I had to get a taxi. Little realising we were 'on the air', I destroyed the myth of Q by saying, 'Sorry I'm late, but the bloody car broke down...' 'Glad you didn't mention our name' said the garage I'd bought it from."

A night at the Lancaster Hotel in London caused Q fresh problems. On driving up to the car park, he inadvertently shoved the ticket in the wrong slot in order to get the barrier to lift. Much to his embarrassment, cars came to a halt behind him and a crowd gathered as they watched the Master of Gadgets wrestle with the complexities of the car park machinery. Unable to get the barrier to respond, he resorted to calling the management and they sorted it out in two minutes! Fortunately he arrived on time at Harrods for a signing session - not of books - but miniatures. "They were incredibly beautiful historical miniatures, made by a firm in Cambridge and used in *The Living Daylights* to depict the Battle of Waterloo. I was given quite a number of them, but God knows where they are today."

At the beginning of 1988, Desmond accepted the role of a detective in *Prisoner of Rio*, a film based coincidentally on Ronnie Biggs. "It was all shot at Pinewood and I had a marvellous part, but for some reason the production was never shown. Still, at least I got paid."

The cash from the film was used for an essential expenditure when Desmond and Pamela celebrated their Golden Wedding at Linkwell in May. The gardens were manicured into shape, the house filled with fresh flowers, a gold and white marquee set up on the lawn and the caterers arrived in full force to ensure all went well on the day. The lengthy guest list was impressively studded with names from the Bond movies as well as family, friends, locals and, "a whole host of other people I didn't know at all." Afterwards, they both escaped to France where it rained constantly for the first few days and Pamela remarked drily, "Fancy coming all this way just to lie on the bed and read."

On returning to England, Desmond made an appointment with a London doctor. Age, angina and general fitness necessitated a routine examination for insurance purposes on Bond No. 16. Everything seemed OK, and Desmond breathed a sigh of relief until the doctor suggested, 'a brisk bit of walking, just to ensure your ticker's in good order'. Fortunately, he failed to notice (or chose not to notice) his patient surreptitiously popping a couple of pills in his mouth before he undertook the test.

In July 1988, Desmond flew to Mexico to film *Licence To Kill*. He returned in August, only to fly out to Mexico again in September, with Pamela, to continue shooting his longest scenes of the entire Bond series.

'Grim', 'Menacing', Believable', 'Notable', 'Controversial', 'Superbly acted, staged and produced', were just some of the critics observations, but for most Bond aficionados, it lacked the accustomed humour and fantasy. Desmond personally found *Licence To Kill* the most rewarding, due to the much extended role of Q, otherwise he felt it was too violent and suggests that several of the brutal scenes were cut altogether. "It's very difficult after 25 years and having a new Bond, not to update things as we head towards the 21st century. It was intended to bring back the basics, but the public preferred the 'larger than life' approach. When people commented to me that 007 is too forbidding in this film, I'd answer, 'well if your best friend had been fed to the sharks and his wife killed on their wedding night, would you go round with a smile on your face?' 'Ah, but Bond would,' they'd reply."

Desmond's few words put the plot of *Licence To Kill* in a nutshell (the original title was *Licence Revoked*). The film begins with the marriage of 007's friend and US counterpart, Felix Leiter. A few hours after the ceremony, Bond returns to the scene of the celebrations and discovers the mutilated body of the bridegroom sprawled across a couch and his wife, of a few hours, lying murdered on the bed. Enraged, he loses all sense of proportion and vows revenge on Franz Sanchez, a ruthless drugs baron, responsible for this unforgivable crime. When M arrives from HQ, he is disturbed to learn of 007's reaction and calls for his Licence to Kill to be revoked. With a stomach punch to M, Bond makes a swift exodus and goes it alone - almost. An anxious and tearful Miss Moneypenny is in her office trying to keep track of him. And Q, showing fatherly concern for this exasperating secret agent, turns up in South America on the pretext of being on holiday, carrying a caseful of essential gadgets for 007.

For the first time in 25 years, Desmond has several significant scenes; his cameo role has grown considerably and it provides a necessary and light-hearted diversion in this production. 007 naturally has a couple of pretty girls vying for his attention: Cary Lowell plays Pam Bouvier, a pilot involved with the CIA, who takes a shine to Bond and becomes his shapely gun-slinging minder. Lupe Lamora, portrayed by Talisa Soto, is Sanchez's mistress who willingly allows herself to be seduced by Bond and then proceeds to fall in love with him. Q is on hand to witness some of the 'faux pas' committed by 007 as he tries to juggle the two women to his advantage in getting a suitable revenge on Sanchez.

The majority of *Licence To Kill* takes place in Florida, South America and, forsaking Pinewood, the Churubusco studios in Mexico City, were used for much of the shooting. Here, according to Desmond, the difficulties such as inefficiency and technical

***Licence To Kill*. Q explains the Hasselblad camera to 007 (Timothy Dalton) as Pam (Cary Lowell) takes an inquisitive peep into his suitcase.**

Q as a road sweeper in *Licence To Kill*.

hitches, never mind the unrelenting boiling weather, were enormous. "In theory, it should have saved a fortune using a 'local' studio. In reality, it probably cost a lot more."

In this film, Q first crops up in the hotel suite platonically shared by 007 and Ms. Bouvier. With him, he carries a suitcase containing 'everything for the man on holiday'. His intrusion is a surprise for Bond who, after heated questioning, tells him to push off back home. Q ignores the remark and with a gentle reminder of, "If it hadn't been for Q branch you'd have been dead long ago," sets to work on the contents of his luggage. To ensure against oversleeping, he'd brought a travelling alarm clock that explodes. He'd also brought a tube of toothpaste packed with explosives and a British passport that detonates on opening. The harmless looking Polaroid camera, which shoots laser beams and takes X-ray pictures, is playfully (mis)used by Pam as she takes it out of Q's case to snap a picture of the two fellas. Just in time, Q gives 007 a shove, they both duck and the laser beam destroys a picture on the wall instead: the priceless look Q bestows on Pam as he snatches the camera away from her, says it all. The real gem from this box of tricks is the Hasselblad camera that can be taken apart and reconstructed as a gun with an optical palm reader, thereby ensuring only Bond can fire the weapon.

When Q has finished his explanatory monologue, Pam sweetly and firmly retires for the night on her own and Q heads off for the twin-bedded room. For a few seconds, 007 is left standing alone, looking non-plussed before he follows the latter, saying in a resigned tone, "I hope you don't snore, Q."

In spite of 007's adamant entreaties about his Gadget Master not being suited to fieldwork, Q hangs around and makes an essential adjunct to Bond's adventures. First he poses as his chauffeur, then a skipper and finally a road sweeper, complete with a straw hat, moustache and a broom containing a walkie-talkie in the handle. In the penultimate scene, he takes on the guise of a benevolent uncle, when he and Pam Bouvier are confronted at the hotel by an agitated Lupe, Sanchez's mistress, telling them she feared 007 was in great danger and she loved him so very much (particularly as he'd just spent the night with her). After Q has tactfully ushered Lupe out of the room, he makes comforting noises to the jealous Pam. For his pains, he's rewarded with a resounding 'Bull Shit'.

It was satisfying for both the actor and his audience to have more screen time and watch Q's crusty character infiltrate other dimensions of the plot as opposed to remaining in the workshop environment. It certainly helped to mitigate some of the seriousness of the film; a feeling shared by the press who referred to him as, 'the pawky septuagenarian Q, plays a wonderfully supportive figure'. 'On Q again for another Bond. We offer our congratulations to the 75 year old Llewelyn in his 14th appearance as Q', wrote one newspaper. 'Bond looks sad as Q takes over'; then *The Telegraph* went on to report, 'supposedly this film was a return to Fleming's gritty realism, but it's not even loosely based on his books. It seems Bond has lost his wry insouciance and, by contrast, as a field operator, Q enjoys his high jinks hugely'. Most critics analysed *Licence To Kill* in depth without any real conclusion except for one that summed it up in eight words, 'a brilliant film, but not a Bond film'.

Yet it was the article in a tabloid newspaper that left Desmond hopping mad. Headed, 'James Bond's boss admits 'I'm skint'', it then continued, 'the world's famous gadget master lives off his government pension, drives a clapped out Renault and only earns a modest daily rate to star in a blockbuster!'. "They twisted absolutely everything", said Desmond, for once looking genuinely irritated. "I merely pointed out I didn't earn the fortune everyone assumes and because I'm so identified with Q, no other work comes in and what cash I get has to last me a long time. That piece

Licence to Kill.

reminded me of Goebbels, Hitler's propaganda master, whose information always contained an element of truth. The rest was distorted out of total recognition."

Although it was generally agreed a Bond film still pulled the audiences, many questioned whether 007's number was up. 'In Roger Moore's day,' commented one fan regretfully, 'Bond would not have gone to the bank and announced, I'm making a withdrawal. Instead, he'd have phoned from the bed, with a blonde beside him, leaving you uncertain if he's referring to banking or bonking!'

The additional wave of attention and pleasing reviews from Q's foray into the world beyond the workshop, left Desmond hoping it would set a precedence for the future 007 movies. He'd grown to enjoy the premieres and increasing publicity tours, television appearances, advertising, radio and speaking engagements resulting from his role as Q. But changes were afoot.

Once again it was time to bid farewell to the familiar and not so familiar faces from Cubby Broccoli's Bond family. The new Miss Moneypenny, Caroline Bliss, had barely had a chance to warm her secretary's chair before she moved on. As did Robert Brown, who had played M so convincingly since *Octopussy*. John Glen, the brilliant director of the last five consecutive Bonds, reckoned it was time for a fresh approach to the productions. Finally, Richard Maibaum, scriptwriter 'extraordinaire' and involved with every 007 movie apart from three, died about a year after *Licence To Kill* was released. It was also questionable whether Timothy Dalton would return as 007 in future. Cubby Broccoli had problems, too.

In a reflective mood on the comings, goings, criticisms and praises of the latest film, Desmond observed, "Richard Maibaum had little to do with the script of *Licence To Kill* which is perhaps the reason why it lacked the fantasy. As I've said before, everything about Bond is larger than life, so, with hindsight, playing him seriously doesn't quite seem to work."

DESMOND LLEWELYN 1305

Production Office: 422 Fleming St., Key West - Florida 33040/Tel.: (305) 292-7600

CINEMA CONSULTANTS, Inc.

"LICENSE REVOKED"

1st Unit CALL SHEET

PLEASE REMEMBER ID's.
NO SMOKING ON PIER.

Call Sheet No. 15

NIGHT SHOOTING

PRODUCERS: **A. R. BROCCOLI**
MICHAEL WILSON

DATE: **THURSDAY - 4th August 1988**

DIRECTOR: **JOHN GLEN**

UNIT CALL: **6.00pm Lv Hotels**
6.15pm On Location

LOCATION: **COAST GUARD H.Q.**
Trumbo Point, Palm Ave.
Delta II North Pier
Key West, FL

|SUNSET: 8.09pm|
|SUNRISE: 6.56am|

Grips/Elec. **5.30pm Lv Hotel**

SETS: **EXT. WAVEKREST/PILOT BOAT - ISTHMUS HARBOUR**

SC. NOS.: **263. 265. 270. 271. 274pt. to comp. 281K. Night.**

ARTISTE	CHARACTER	D/ROOM	P/UP	M-UP/HAIR/WDBE	ON SET
TIMOTHY DALTON	James Bond	Trailer	8.15pm	8.30pm	9.00pm
CAREY LOWELL	Pam	Motorhome	7.30pm	7.45pm	9.00pm
ROBERT DAVI	Sanchez	Motorhome	S/by @ hotel from 6.00pm.		
TALISA SOTO	Lupe	Motorhome	S/by @ hotel from 6.00pm.		
ANTHONY ZERBE	Krest	Motorhome	6.45pm	7.00pm	7.45pm
DON STROUD	Heller	Honeywagon	To be advised.		
ALEJANDRO BRACHO	Perez	Honeywagon	S/by @ hotel from 6.00pm.		
GUY DE SAINT CYR	Braun	Honeywagon	S/by @ hotel from 6.00pm.		
DESMOND LLEWELYN	Q	Motorhome	8.15pm	8.30pm	9.00pm
ROGER CUDNEY	Capt/Mate	Honeywagon	S/by @ hotel from 6.00pm.		

Stand-ins/Doubles:

DEL BRIKEY	For Mr. Dalton	6.00pm	6.15pm	As req.
CHRISTINE BERG	For Ms. Lowell	6.00pm	6.15pm	As req.
A. N. OTHER	For Mr. Zerbe	6.00pm	6.15pm	As req.
A. N. OTHER (MALE)	Utility	6.00pm	6.15pm	As req.

OTHER STAND-INS To be advised on completion of shooting (Thursday A.M.).

Boat Driving Doubles:

WILLIAM CROSCUP	For "Q" on Pilot Boat		6.15pm	As req.
JOE NEWHOUSE	For "Capt" on Wavekrest		6.15pm	As req.

Crowd:

10 MEN	Wavekrest Crew	6.00pm	6.15pm	As req.
10 MEN	Isthmus Soldiers	To be advised.		
1 MAN	Sanchez's Limo Driver	To be advised.		

Stunt Co-ordinator: As per PAUL WESTON

Stunt Doubles:

SIMON CRANE	For James Bond	Honeywagon	6.00pm	6.15pm	As req.

Marine Co-ordinator: As per LARRY HILLS

Desmond's Call Sheet for filming *Licence To Kill* - Original title *License Revoked*

- 10 -

A MAN CALLED Q

A moment of contemplation whilst filming *Tomorrow Never Dies*. 1997.

"Inevitably, Q has taken over my life,
but I think it's really longevity which is
responsible for all the fame."

- 10 -
A MAN CALLED Q

Since *Octopussy*, Desmond no longer regards Q as a backroom boffin, but a kind of travelling straight man for 007 to bounce his quips off - and supply his gadgets. Not strictly true, but it's a curious role to define. Q is not a funny man, in fact, quite the opposite, despite the fact that his appearance evokes a ready smile and a hidden chuckle. Perhaps it's the gruff pathos that Desmond has incorporated into Q which has made him such an appealing character. His facial expressions, when confronted by the charming, but aggravating, 007, are amusing and self- explanatory. The words are almost unnecessary. Here is a man dedicated to the compilation and use of lethal gadgetry having to cope with a secret agent who, in his opinion, treats life, women and most importantly, his equipment, with blithe disregard. Yet, there is also something unforgettable about Q's lines; not what he says, but how he says them.

His voice is distinctive. Long after a Bond film has finished, his comments linger. Perhaps this is one of the indefinable factors that contribute to Desmond's enormous popularity. Whatever, it's certainly not due to lengthy appearances. By the beginning of the 1990's, Q's total screen time amounted to just half an hour. For a back room boffin to achieve stardom from 30 minutes, spread over roughly the same number of years, must be one of the most unique situations in show business.

In the summer of 1989, Desmond's son, Justin, re-married. "To a lovely girl called Clare, who invited some of her stunning friends to the wedding. They'd knock spots off any of the Bond girls, except that they were a horsy crowd and all had handshakes like navvies." Ivor, the bachelor of the family, celebrated his fortieth birthday and then confounded everybody by marrying a few months later. His marriage to Georgia took place north of the border, in Edinburgh. "It was a wonderfully memorable occasion and Pamela and I were both delighted to see him settle down."

Spasmodic requests to undertake things unrelated to Bond sometimes cropped up. As the guest speaker at an 'Artificial Sweetener' Conference in Cannes, Desmond's usual ebullience became sorely dented. "It was a bit unnerving as I had all these lines to learn about a product I knew nothing about. I found it extremely difficult without a prompt at hand and I buggered the whole thing up. Somebody did suggest to me afterwards that I might have a mild form of dyslexia, but I guess it's old age." However, a gardening show in Birmingham restored his self-assurance as he explained every garden gadget without a hitch. "Afterwards, I clearly remember talking to a funny little man from one newspaper, who was amused at my lack of technical skills. Pamela said to me later, 'You must stop calling people, regardless of their stature, funny little men.' She was right. Particularly as in this incident, I discovered it was Rupert Murdoch!"

Talking about gadgets at an Electrical Convention in Las Vegas followed and from there Desmond travelled to Toronto and attended the Toronto Boat Show, where all the Bond boats were on display. Whilst signing autographs, he received the inevitable question, "When's the next 007 movie coming out?" "Hopefully soon," came back Q's non-committal reply.

Where was James Bond at the beginning of the 1990's? "At present in limbo," so Desmond learned from Cubby Broccoli, who implied there was a slight problem between EON Productions and MGM/UA. But the slight problem proved excessively

With the family, including grandchildren, at Linkwell. From left to right:- Pamela, Georgia, Desmond, Clare, Justin and Ivor (seated).

complicated and required lawyers and lawsuits. It would take three years of wearisome litigation before everything had been resolved and until then there would be no Bond. Cubby faced a stressful and unproductive future, although his family and extraordinarily optimistic personality stood him in good stead.

Michael G. Wilson, Cubby's stepson, provided valuable support. He had become a part of the Broccoli family when his mother, Dana, married Cubby in 1960. After a brief flirtation with the production of *Goldfinger*, he continued his career as an eminently successful lawyer until the mid-70s. He then became an assistant to the producer on *The Spy Who Loved Me* and executive producer on *Moonraker, For Your Eyes Only* and *Octopussy*. After earning his stripes from these films, he became Cubby's partner in *A View To A Kill, The Living Daylights* and *Licence To Kill*. He also collaborated with Richard Maibaum on five of the screenplays.

Barbara Broccoli, Cubby and Dana's daughter, grew up with James Bond. There is never a moment when the secret agent hasn't been a part of her life; Desmond can still recall her being brought to the studios as a little girl. After gaining a degree in Motion Picture and Television Communications, Barbara worked as an assistant director on *Octopussy* and *A View To A Kill*. As an associate producer on *The Living Daylights* and *Licence To Kill* she proved to everybody she was truly her father's daughter.

The presence of Dana, whilst often not mentioned, was no less important. When reading Cubby's autobiography, the closeness of their relationship soon becomes apparent as well as her strong influence on Cubby's decisions. "She's a lovely, wise lady," comments Desmond, who has known her for many years. "I've always reckoned the Broccolis are not a business, but a family and that includes everybody involved in the James Bond productions." It was with this clan firmly behind him that Cubby withstood the protracted months of litigation.

Naturally, Desmond felt uncertain, and at one point had serious doubts, if there would be any further 007 movies. Nevertheless, financially, he suddenly found himself in clover. His agent, Rebecca Blond, at Rebecca Blond Associates, had secured a contract for him in Detroit to film an advertisement. "It was three or four days of bloody hard work, portraying Q supposedly selling equipment at an exhibition. I was exhausted afterwards - but earning a staggering £65,000 made it all very worth while. Believe it or not, the next year I was asked to reproduce the same performance for another £65,000. Expecting a once a year repeat, I thought I was made for life. Unfortunately, the firm went bankrupt."

In 1991, just when a new Bond should have been under way, Desmond sought the advice of a heart specialist after reading of a new technique in heart surgery; he'd also realised that pill-popping was no longer as effective in masking angina. After a thorough examination and several tests, the specialist told him what he'd already guessed. It was time for a heart by-pass operation.

With complete faith in the medical profession, Desmond approached his operation with all the spirit of going on holiday, even down to obtaining a package deal for one week's stay in a private hospital. The operation, a triple by-pass, proved a great success and afterwards, the patient said, "I felt absolutely no pain whatsoever and now I'm a new man." Nevertheless, convalescence took a little longer than expected and Desmond found himself totally hooked on watching television 'soaps'. Some months elapsed before he finally felt fit enough to embark on two days work on an unremembered film *October 32nd* ! "It took place in Greenwich and I think I had a few lines as an astronomer. I know the cameraman and the director fought like hell all the time."

Shortly after, an advertisement for yoghurt in Dublin provided a paid stopping point on the way to Co. Mayo for a holiday. One man who watched Desmond's scene being filmed said to him afterwards. "My God, if only you could have seen your face screw up in disgust when you first tasted that yoghurt."

Whilst there were no Bond movies in the pipeline, *Thirty Years of James Bond*, a television documentary, kept 007 in the public eye. It brought back memories, highlighted the action-packed suspense from all 16 films and examined some of the narrow escapes ensuing from stunt work. It also featured the more outstanding gadgets accompanied by due comment from Q.

In October 1992, Desmond took on his most daunting assignment associated with Bond so far. At Earls Court, a tribute entitled, *Forty Glorious Years*, celebrated the fortieth anniversary of the Queen's Accession. Highlighting events from all those years were a wide gathering of performers and Q represented the Bond films. His brief was simple; just drive the Aston Martin slowly past the Queen. "I was terrified as the car was pretty ancient and I had no idea how reliable it would be. Knowing my luck, I was convinced the car would konk out and I'd have to push the thing past Her Majesty."

As the months rolled by, the idea of playing Q again became more remote. A few things cropped up: a part in BBC's *Sherlock Holmes*, an amateur video, Charles Fraser-Smith's exhibition at Dover Castle, more advertisements, but even they were dwindling.

An exhibition of Corgi Toys in Birmingham re-awakened Q's gadget master instincts when he autographed dozens of boxed Bond cars. The venue also presented the chance for Desmond to meet Honor Blackman (Pussy Galore in *Goldfinger*); one of his favourite Bond women. As both stood obligingly in front of the Aston Martin, Little Nellie and the Lotus to be photographed, he had a sudden conviction that 007 would shortly return to the screen. He was right. By the time 1993 drew to a close, the 17th Bond had reached the drawing board.

Around this time Pamela and Desmond made the sensible, but heartbreaking, decision to leave Linkwell. There were contributing factors, not least two people bordering on 80 rattling around in a seven-bedroomed house. It seemed only sensible to let Ivor, now he was married with a family, move into Linkwell. It also coincided with the property opposite coming up for sale. "Osborn House was a lovely little place; small by comparison, but perfectly adequate. The move was so easy - we just carried the furniture across the road. But Pamela never seemed to settle. I think the wrench of leaving Linkwell upset her more than anybody realised, even though it had ultimately been her choice to do so. Shortly after the move, she fell downstairs and broke her hip. That probably added to her disorientation."

By the summer of 1994, Desmond, much to his incredulity, had been asked to play Q in *Goldeneye*. "I was ecstatic and very honoured, having been the only one asked to return from the eighties era. Timothy had withdrawn from his role as Bond, by mutual agreement, and Pierce Brosnan had, at long last, stepped in as 007. I also learned Judi Dench had been asked to play M. I wondered if the original Miss Moneypenny, Lois Maxwell, had instigated the idea of M being a woman. Apparently, Lois had asked Cubby, ten years earlier, if she could play M and he'd said, 'No, it was unthinkable to have M as a woman.' How times have changed."

Whilst on holiday in Ireland that same year, a disturbing incident occurred when Desmond and Pamela stayed with friends. On going to bed that night, Pamela appeared to be rather odd and at first Desmond assumed she'd had too much to drink; although he admitted that would be very unlike her. "She seemed lost and couldn't

With Honor Blackman at an exhibition in Birmingham 1993. In the foreground the Aston Martin; behind, Little Nellie and the Lotus.

find her way around or remember where everything was kept, but by the next day she was alright again - or so I thought. On the homeward journey she appeared irritable and displayed an unusual fit of temper when I got lost, trying to take a short cut."

As new faces were sought for *Goldeneye*, so an old one passed on. Terence Young, the director of *Dr. No, From Russia With Love* and *Thunderball* died at the age of 80. He did much towards the fashioning of Bond movies, and without him there would not have been the Q we know today. Saddened, Desmond attended the memorial service, but cannot remember if Pamela accompanied him.

"There was no doubt her odd spells were getting more frequent. Sometimes she'd get very angry and accuse me of having an affair. I think she was muddling me up with her father. I got so desperate at one stage, I went and fetched two photographs, one of myself and one of her father. I showed them to her and said, 'Just point to the one you think is me,' and she put her finger firmly on her father's picture. Then she'd go back to being perfectly normal and I'd try to convince myself that it was nothing to worry about. But, we were all very concerned."

The preparations to launch the new James Bond went ahead once Pierce Brosnan had undergone the initiation formalities. At 42, and a Bond fan since schooldays, Pierce was enormously pleased to have a crack at the role he'd so narrowly lost in 1986.

His introduction to the world media took place at the newly constructed 007 Studio just outside London at Leavesden - the Pinewood studio being unavailable for filming. Here, amongst cameras and questions, Desmond met him for the first time. "It was a fantastic occasion. After five years without a Bond the atmosphere was, as you can imagine, euphoric. Everybody was there: cast, crew, producers, directors, personalities, press and TV. Pierce, of course, was surrounded and I only chatted to him for a few minutes, but we got on very well."

There was just one person notably absent from these festivities - Cubby Broccoli. Now in his mid-80s and having undergone intensive heart surgery, he remained at home in Beverly Hills, with Dana, and looked after by nurses. The highly complex logistics of producing *Goldeneye* lay with Michael G. Wilson and Barbara Broccoli.

The filming of *Goldeneye*, named after Ian Fleming's retreat in Jamaica, began in the early spring of 1995. Although the ingredients carried the nineties updating, the production remained basically unchanged. Desmond, appearing with Pierce for the first time, thought he made an excellent Bond and furnished the character with the right amount of steely wit. He also found him a comfortable person to work with. This was evident from the film when Q's crusty persona bears a hint of relaxed joviality as 007 pays the routine call to his workshop. When Q appears in a wheelchair with his leg in a plaster cast and 007 shows due concern, he responds with a suggestion of a grin and demonstrates the cast's capabilities as a rocket launcher. He then hops out of the chair with the agility of a teenager, before introducing Bond to his new car.

This time it's a BMW Z3 Roadster and with the customary, "Now pay attention, 007," Q explains the Stinger missiles, a radar system and a parachute that billows out from the back of the car. As his listener appears to be considering a joyride, Q remonstrates, "Need I remind you, 007, you have a licence to kill, not to break the traffic laws."

Amongst the noise and action of Q's workshop, Bond is shown his next piece of equipment; a leather belt with a piton in the buckle and a 75 foot reinforced rappelling cord. Q's following gadget is a slender pen which, after a few clicks, changes into a Class 4 grenade. This gives rise to a comment about 'the writing being on the wall', before Desmond has the chance to add his very own, written-in, one-liner.

The new 007, Pierce Brosnan watches Q demonstrate his leg cast rocket launcher in *Goldeneye.*

"Don't say it - the writing's on the wall!" *Goldeneye.*

"Oh, do grow up, 007." Having been given the usual salutary reminder of, "returning all the equipment in pristine condition," 007 is about to make an exit when he sees a filled bread roll on the side. As he examines this novel gadget, Q's smile fades and he grabs it from 007's hands. "Don't touch that," he exclaims with a touch of his old irritability, "that's my lunch."

In spite of the joys of playing Q, together with the related spin-offs, Desmond found life slightly onerous. Pamela was difficult and as the pre-launch publicity of the new film approached, he knew he couldn't leave her alone. Ivor and Georgia were unhesitating; she must stay at Linkwell whilst he went to America for Bond.

In November, the day before the premiere of *Goldeneye*, Pierce and Desmond faced, for the umpteenth time, a battery of press, cameras and questions. Later that evening, as Desmond relaxed with some of the cast at The Hyde Park Hotel, Pierce suddenly walked across and gave his shoulder an affectionate squeeze. "I thought the man had gone quite mad. I'd been working with him all day and now he was hugging me as though we hadn't met for years." The cause of Pierce's burst of affection soon manifested itself. As Desmond turned, he saw Michael Aspel purposefully approaching him, clutching a large red book. "Desmond Llewelyn - This is Your Life."

"My reaction, apart from surprise, was one of complete panic. Oh Christ, I thought, what about Pamela? How will she cope? Will she be alright? Silly of me really, as Ivor and Justin were obviously aware of the programme and they would look after her. I later discovered they'd planned it all from the beginning. Thankfully, when I reached Teddington Studios and walked apprehensively on to *This Is Your Life*, I saw Pamela sitting quietly by the boys."

For the next half-an-hour, friends past and present recalled events as Desmond's life unfolded. Jo Bailey, an ex-Radlean, embarked on an outrageous tale about rugger, to which Desmond counteracted, impishly, "If I may say so, that's absolute balls." Derek Tansley recollected their days together in repertory with Matthew Forsyth; Lord Peyton, the wartime story of the tunnel at Warburg. Lois Maxwell, John Glen and Pierce Brosnan related a few incidents from Bond. Michael G. Wilson and Barbara Broccoli sat amongst the guests. The latest Bond girls, whom Desmond had never met, came on and asked which was his favourite gadget? He shrugged his shoulders and put his hands up in mock despair, "Frankly," he said, "I hate bloody gadgets."

"I enjoyed the party afterwards much more than the programme. After all, *This Is Your Life* is a bit false and guests say silly things. I think it would be much better if there wasn't all this damn secrecy and then it could be more relaxed."

The crowds that gathered for the premiere of *Goldeneye* were larger than ever. It seemed the five year gap had not diminished the appeal of James Bond, nor of Q. If anything, the popularity of this octogenarian actor had snowballed and the critics gave almost as much coverage to Q as the new 007. Desmond refers to the hype as 'the Q factor'. "It's incredible. But it's only because I've been in every Bond, except two, since the beginning and fans look on me as some sort of gadget-minded icon. Really, it's all down to longevity!"

Ironically, at 81, Desmond was about to embark on the most productive years of his entire career. When many have retired to grow cabbages, he would flit around the world and undertake a variety of glamourous commitments in the name of Q. Feeling that Desmond should have a minder on his globe trotting engagements, EON assigned Amanda Schofield, from their publicity department, as a chaperone. Desmond's comments on her company brought a twinkle to his eye. "Oh, if only I were younger. She really is the most enchanting woman."

In January, Q's presence was requested in Las Vegas where, in one day alone, Desmond signed 1,000 signatures. Then it was off to Sweden, Germany, Dublin and

Desmond, having just been informed by Michael Aspel - *This Is Your Life.*

France where he should have attended *The World of James Bond* at the Paris Motor Show. Unfortunately, severe complications resulting from a hiatus hernia rushed him back to the Conquest Hospital in Hastings. "They were marvellous." Once on his feet again, he continued his travels and undertook several TV appearances, including the *Esther Rantzen Show*, countless radio programmes and the unveiling of a memorial plaque to Ian Fleming in London.

At home, events took on a more sombre note when, in April, Desmond consulted doctors about Pamela's deteriorating capabilities. "It was a dreadful moment when I learned that the tests carried out revealed Alzheimer's. Here was this lovely, capable, intelligent woman being snatched from me in all but her physical person. We - Justin, Ivor and the rest of the family - decided that, for the moment, we could cope by sharing the burden of looking after her. Even so, it was difficult. One had to watch Pamela the whole time in case she let herself out of the front door and, unable to remember where she lived, simply disappeared. After a particularly fraught holiday in Ireland, it became evident to all of us that she needed round-the-clock care. The rapid progression of Alzheimer's had disallowed her any form of remission.

"It was a glorious autumn morning in October 1996 when I took Pamela into the nursing home. She followed me like a lamb - poor love - and appeared to be happy with her surroundings, which helped me a bit. Nevertheless, I felt dreadful, particularly when I got back to Osborn House later that day and saw all her belongings in their usual place, as though she was about to return. The one small shred of comfort was the fact that the nursing home was situated nearby and I could pop round and see her every day. Initially, I found the most frustrating thing about Alzheimer's was the total inability for either of us to communicate on any level. In desperation, I'd search for signs of recognition, a glimmer of a memory, a sensible sentence from non-sensical words. Now I've learned to accept the situation and I just tell Pamela what I've been doing, give her a hug and then leave, not knowing if she's understood a word. But she seems content enough in her entirely private world."

Desmond's pragmatic character ensured he counted his blessings instead of dwelling on, "a perfectly beastly October", although he was unusually reflective when he contemplated the past months. "You see, before Pamela was really ill there was Cubby's funeral. But, I'm luckier than most, I've two wonderful sons, four super grandchildren... and Bond."

Cubby Broccoli died at his home in Beverly Hills in June 1996. He was 87. To the millions he'd never met, he left a legacy of unrepeatable screen thrillers. To his family and friends, he left an irreplaceable void. Fortunately, his unequivocal enthusiasm for producing James Bond movies manifested itself in his stepson and daughter and when Cubby learned *Goldeneye* had grossed 350 million dollars, he knew his 'baby' lay in the best possible hands.

Desmond was present at both Cubby's funeral, a celebration of his life, and the internment afterwards. "It was an incredibly moving occasion, accentuated by a perfect summer's day and the distinguished actor, Gregory Peck, who spoke eloquently about his memories of Cubby. Timothy Dalton joined the family as a pallbearer. There were so many stars who wanted to pay their last respects to such a great man and friend. It was truly the passing of an era. I was particularly touched when Barbara included me in the family dinner the night before the funeral." Fittingly, Cubby Broccoli's memorial service took place at The Odeon, Leicester Square, the following November.

With an increasing passion for his Welsh background, Desmond accepted two separate requests to appear in amateur videos without hesitation. Both had the ring of nostalgia. The first, *Taboo*, was produced by the students of E Social at Radley College. By sheer coincidence the filming took place at Penhow, where Desmond, as a boy, attended church every Sunday with his parents. This was primarily because his Aunt Elenita had been the wife of the Vicar of Penhow. The second video, *Watching The Wheels*, was the product of a film school in Newport. One scene Desmond found particularly sentimental features him with a bicycle by the canal that runs at the bottom of the garden at Blaen-y-pant.

Recently, the past caught up with him again when he returned to Robecq, the scene of his capture in 1940. Together with Mike Edwards, another ex-officer from the 1st Battalion of The Royal Welch Fusiliers, they retraced their wartime route but found the familiar landmarks had disappeared and the area changed out of recognition.

Bond No. 18, *Tomorrow Never Dies*, got under way in the spring of 1997. As with many epic productions, it was not without problems. The primary dilemma was caused by Pinewood being unable to accommodate such a blockbuster and Leavesden Studios, used for the previous film, being taken up with *Star Wars*. A third, and new, studio had to be created from an abandoned warehouse in Hertfordshire. It left the shortest time yet for shooting.

Desmond's scenes were filmed on location at Hamburg and Stanstead. Both were with Pierce Brosnan (007), who, Desmond reckoned, "was very patient with me as I kept on fumbling my lines. I blamed the director, because he wouldn't let me use 'idiot boards'. I warned him it would take hours - and it did."

Again, one of Q's gadgets in *Tomorrow Never Dies*, is an Omega watch, this time containing a detonator with an ignition system in the rotary face. Disappointingly, Desmond did not receive another invitation to dine with the head of Omega as he had done when one of their watches featured in *Goldeneye*. "It was at his chalet by Lake Lausanne, a fantastic place and the host, whose name escapes me, showed me his vast wine cellar. Having asked me my birth date, he then gave me a bottle of wine of the same vintage. I've still got the bottle - empty, of course." Ericsson Telephones also provided a round of appearances for Q. One of their portable models contained a few of his extras and, in the new film, allowed 007 complete control of his new BMW, even if he's not in the driving seat!

Before the premiere of *Tomorrow Never Dies*, Desmond was questioned on a TV interview about the content of the plot. Momentarily he looked flummoxed, then replied with an engaging smile, "Well y'know - the same as usual, but noisier." This time, the story concerned the media megalomaniac, Elliot Carver, provoking international tragedies to ensure his news empire was first in the race of world-wide broadcasting. Amidst a lot of fracas, an overlong motorcycle chase and the help of Wai Lin, a Chinese agent, 007 got to grips with his new assignment and ensured Carver met his doom.

For the second time, Judi Dench returned to play a convincing M. "She is such a wonderfully professional actress. I met her husband, Michael, when she was initially being considered for the role and he said to me, 'Judi's been asked if she'd like to play M. She's frightfully excited, but do you think she'll get it?' Of course she'll get it, I replied, amused by the inconceivable idea that anybody should think otherwise."

Samantha Bond made another appearance as Miss Moneypenny and, as ever, Q was there, indomitable, immortal and, allegedly innovative - his guns, gadgets and vehicles, in reality created by the special effects team, yet again got Bond out of crises.

As in some of the previous movies, Q had to trek round the globe to hand over the equipment to 007. In *Tomorrow Never Dies*, this took place at Hamburg Airport and Q was in the guise of an Avis Car Hire employee, complete with a bright red jacket, "which I loathed." His lines - so tedious when rehearsing - slipped easily off the tongue, and were a touch sarcastic as he walked with Bond to the hangar containing his new BMW 750. Naturally, Q had equipped the vehicle with one or two tricks. There's the bullet proof glass and bodywork, self inflating tyres and, concealed in the sunroof are a few rockets. But that wasn't all. A tear gas mechanism, metal spikes concealed behind the rear bumper and a 20,000 volt shock system, a security against forced entry, almost completed the picture until Q demonstrated his trump card - the remote control gadget.

This was hidden in an Ericsson cellular telephone which, when opened, held a close circuit TV monitor to enable 007 to see where the car was going. It also contained the activator for the security system. Unable to resist the temptation of a driverless vehicle, 007 gave the remote control pad a little bit of fingertip acceleration and after a spin, he brought the car to a grinding halt, inches from Q's foot. Q was not amused. Nonetheless, he continued to supply 007 with the rest of his equipment: an updated model of the Walter PPK - the P99 and a Dunhill cigarette lighter which became a grenade at the flick of a switch.

Immediately after the premiere of *Tomorrow Never Dies*, Desmond was in constant demand at different venues all over the world. Once again, his scrambled thoughts are intermittently jotted in his diary:-

> No Royals at Premiere this time, but Ivor and Justin came instead. Party at Bedford Square - covered by a tent. Attended by over 1,000, met Diana's butler. Copenhagen. Treated like VIP, Amanda travelling with me - party afterwards - bit tired - didn't attend. Stockholm. Antwerp. Wonderful suite, beautiful architecture, party for 600. Amsterdam. Same procedure. Visited Anne Frank's house. Oslo Premiere. Streets closed and army helicopters fly overhead. Military escorts made us feel like royalty. Nowhere to hang things. Just remembered, good Irish pub in Amsterdam that had my Guinness. Interview in Houses of Parliament. Interview with *Hello* magazine. Television. Frankfurt for Bond exhibition. Got £3000. America for Ericsson. Autographs all the time. Wore my old tweed suit - Americans love it. Did spoof Bond in Miami. Signed 1,000 autographs in Dallas. Chat show in Chicago.

Over the last two years, in Q related appearances, Desmond has been to America six or seven times, Germany four, Scandinavia three, Amsterdam and France twice, Estonia, Russia, Japan and South Africa, once. Within four hours of his return from South Africa, he flew to Edinburgh for Scottish Telecom. "If only Pamela could see what all 'this bloody Bond rubbish' has led to. Every time I visit, I faithfully tell her all about it. Do you know," and here his voice trails off a bit, "when I went to see her last week, I put my arm round her and said, 'Pamela, guess what today is - it's our wedding anniversary - our 60th - Diamond, I think.' Her lovely eyes just gazed at me blankly, no recognition - nothing. It's a terrible illness."

As the millennium approaches, there is an inexplicable upsurge in everything associated with James Bond - and Q. Perhaps the Christie's Auction of Bond Memorabilia in 1998 highlighted the increasing attention to this screen phenomenon. Momentarily, Desmond, who attended the sale, considered selling the suit he was wearing on the assumption that the price it would have fetched should have given him enough cash to buy another four suits. However, avid autograph hunters caused Q to make a rapid exit through the stockroom, before he'd even taken his jacket off.

Back home from his travels yet again, Desmond is delighted to report that he's been working on a film called, *Error 2000*, in Germany. It has nothing whatsoever to do

Trying out the capabilities of the remote control system for 007's new BMW. ***Tomorrow Never Dies.***

Desmond at the premiere of *Tomorrow Never Dies*, with Jonathan Pryce who portrayed Elliot Carver in the film.

with Q and he plays a professor who is deeply concerned with the Millennium Bug.

But Q is never far away and Desmond admits the character has become an integral part of his everyday life, as well as giving him a future. An exhibition entitled *Licence To Thrill* has opened at The Trocadero in Leicester Square. For a few pounds, visitors can partake in the Bond experience and be briefed by M and Q - the latter being Guest of Honour at the official opening in August 1999. In January 2000, there is a television documentary on Desmond's life from his Welsh background to the present day. In between times, Bond No. 19 will have reached the cinemas.

Directed by Michael Apted (who worked with Desmond on *Follyfoot*), *The World Is Not Enough* has, Desmond thinks, "Something to do with oil and The Caspian Sea." His repeated request for Q to have an assistant has finally materialised and the role of R is played by John Cleese. Q's equipment includes yet another new car for 007 and this time it's a BMW (Z8) - the absolute latest in intercepts, surveillance and countermeasures.

Ivor and Justin are justifiably proud of their father's achievements. Yet, Desmond, at home and surrounded by the chaos of fan mail, photographs and a video recorder that's gone on the blink, is perplexed by all the attention directed at Q. Will the world's most illustrious Gadget Master be in Bond No. 20? His air of rumpled surprise is genuine as he replies with a roguish smile, "Of course, just so long as EON want me and The Almighty doesn't."

***The World Is Not Enough*. Q introduces R (John Cleese) to 007 (Pierce Brosnan).**

On the set of *'The World Is Not Enough'*.

- 11 -

A COMPREHENSIVE LIST OF Q's GADGETRY

1985, 007 with his backroom allies. From left to right. Roger Moore, Desmond , Geoffrey Keen (Frederick Gray, Minister of Defence), Robert Brown (M) and Lois Maxwell (Miss Moneypenny).

"I hate gadgets.
As soon as I touch them,
they go wrong."

DR. NO - 1962.

Producers -	ALBERT R. BROCCOLI AND HARRY SALTZMAN
Director -	TERENCE YOUNG
007 -	SEAN CONNERY
M -	BERNARD LEE
Major Boothroyd -	PETER BURTON
Miss Moneypenny -	LOIS MAXWELL

GADGETRY

- **Q** In this film Major Boothroyd, played by Peter Burton was the official armourer, responsible for getting Bond to change his Beretta .22 for a Walter PPK. Apart from a Geiger Counter, gadgetry is not a feature.

FROM RUSSIA WITH LOVE - 1963.

Producers -	ALBERT R. BROCCOLI AND HARRY SALTZMAN
Director -	TERENCE YOUNG
007 -	SEAN CONNERY
M -	BERNARD LEE
Major Boothroyd -	DESMOND LLEWELYN
Miss Moneypenny -	LOIS MAXWELL

GADGETRY

- **Q** Desmond Llewelyn takes over the role of Major Boothroyd, who has now become the head of Q Branch.
- **Q** The famous briefcase containing 50 gold sovereigns, two tubes of ammunition, two knives, a magnetized tin of talcum powder concealing a tear gas cartridge and an AR7 - a folding sniper's rifle. The briefcase locks had to be turned horizontally prior to opening, otherwise the tear gas cartridge would explode.
- **Q** A special Rolleiflex camera with a recording device.
- **Q** A bleeper to warn 007 of incoming calls.

GOLDFINGER - 1964.

Producers -	ALBERT R. BROCCOLI AND HARRY SALTZMAN
Director -	GUY HAMILTON
007 -	SEAN CONNERY
M -	BERNARD LEE
Boothroyd/Q -	DESMOND LLEWELYN
Miss Moneypenny -	LOIS MAXWELL

GADGETRY

- **Q** The legendary Aston Martin DB5 is introduced with, machine guns, oil dispenser concealed in rear lights, rear smoke screen, bullet proof shields, revolving number plates, passenger ejector seat, nail dispenser, saw blade from wheel hubs and homer terminal.

- Homers/receivers.
- Tear gas parking meter.
- Machine gun dummy in Post Office van.
- Timing device with plastic explosive.
- Bullet proof vest.
- Seagull snorkel/dry suit.
- Grappling hook gun.

THUNDERBALL - 1965.

Presenters -	ALBERT R. BROCCOLI AND HARRY SALTZMAN
Producer -	KEVIN McCLORY
Director -	TERENCE YOUNG
007 -	SEAN CONNERY
M -	BERNARD LEE
Q -	DESMOND LLEWELYN
Miss Moneypenny -	LOIS MAXWELL

GADGETRY

- By this film Q had firmly replaced the name Major Boothroyd.
- 007's Aston Martin - as previously.
- Bell Textron Rocket Belt (jet pack).
- Miniaturized breathing apparatus (sub aqua).
- Bond's underwater breathing pack with motor, dye container, two compressed air missiles with explosive heads.
- Underwater camera.
- Geiger Counter watch.
- Sea - air rescue raft.
- Radioactive pill and mini flare device.
- Dictionary tape deck.

YOU ONLY LIVE TWICE - 1967.

Producers -	ALBERT R. BROCCOLI AND HARRY SALTZMAN
Director -	LEWIS GILBERT
007 -	SEAN CONNERY
M -	BERNARD LEE
Q -	DESMOND LLEWELYN
Miss Moneypenny -	LOIS MAXWELL

GADGETRY

- Gyrocopter named 'Little Nellie' with, two rocket launchers firing heat seeking air-to-air missiles, two flame throwers, two machine guns, smoke ejectors and aerial mines launched by parachutes.

- Flight helmet containing a camera.
- Cigarette with rocket powered dart.
- Special breathing shroud in sea burial.
- Safe decoder which runs through every code.

ON HER MAJESTY'S SECRET SERVICE - 1969.

Producers -	ALBERT R. BROCCOLI AND HARRY SALTZMAN
Director -	PETER HUNT
007 -	GEORGE LAZENBY
M -	BERNARD LEE
Q -	DESMOND LLEWELYN
Miss Moneypenny -	LOIS MAXWELL

GADGETRY

- New Aston Martin DB5.
- Special Armalite machine gun.
- Radio-active fluff in a small box.
- Box containing computerised safe opener and copying machine.
- Minox B camera.

DIAMONDS ARE FOR EVER - 1971.

Producers -	ALBERT R. BROCCOLI AND HARRY SALTZMAN
Director -	GUY HAMILTON
007 -	SEAN CONNERY
M -	BERNARD LEE
Q -	DESMOND LLEWELYN
Miss Moneypenny -	LOIS MAXWELL

GADGETRY

- Special voice simulator or 'voice box' for changing voices and imitating others.
- Device for winning jackpots on fruit machines.
- Holster finger clamp kept in Bond's jacket.
- Piton gun.
- Latex fingerprints.

LIVE AND LET DIE - 1973.

Producers -	ALBERT R. BROCCOLI AND HARRY SALTZMAN
Director -	GUY HAMILTON
007 -	ROGER MOORE
M -	BERNARD LEE
Miss Moneypenny -	LOIS MAXWELL

GADGETRY

- Q does not appear in person in this film, but a few of his gadgets still feature.
- Special shark gun.
- High pressure capsules which blow up the victim.
- Magnetic watch (Rolex).
- Circular saw on watch.
- Special bug detector in toilet kit.
- Hairbrush transmitter.

THE MAN WITH A GOLDEN GUN - 1974.

Producers -	ALBERT R. BROCCOLI AND HARRY SALTZMAN
Director -	GUY HAMILTON
007 -	ROGER MOORE
M -	BERNARD LEE
Q -	DESMOND LLEWELYN
Miss Moneypenny -	LOIS MAXWELL

GADGETRY

- Nikon camera which caused subject to explode when aimed.
- Homing device and detector.
- A 'third' nipple.

THE SPY WHO LOVED ME - 1977.

Producer -	ALBERT R. BROCCOLI
Director -	LEWIS GILBERT
007 -	ROGER MOORE
M -	BERNARD LEE
Q -	DESMOND LLEWELYN
Miss Moneypenny-	LOIS MAXWELL
Frederick Gray -	GEOFFREY KEEN

GADGETRY

- Bond's new car is a Lotus Esprit, capable of becoming a submarine equipped to fire underwater missiles and sea-to-air missiles from the car bonnet. It also had a rear cement spray and oil release mechanism.
- Ski pole rifle.
- Special parachute rig for pre-title sequence.
- Wet bike.
- Cigarette case converted into a microfile viewer.
- Special Seiko watch with ticker-tape read off.

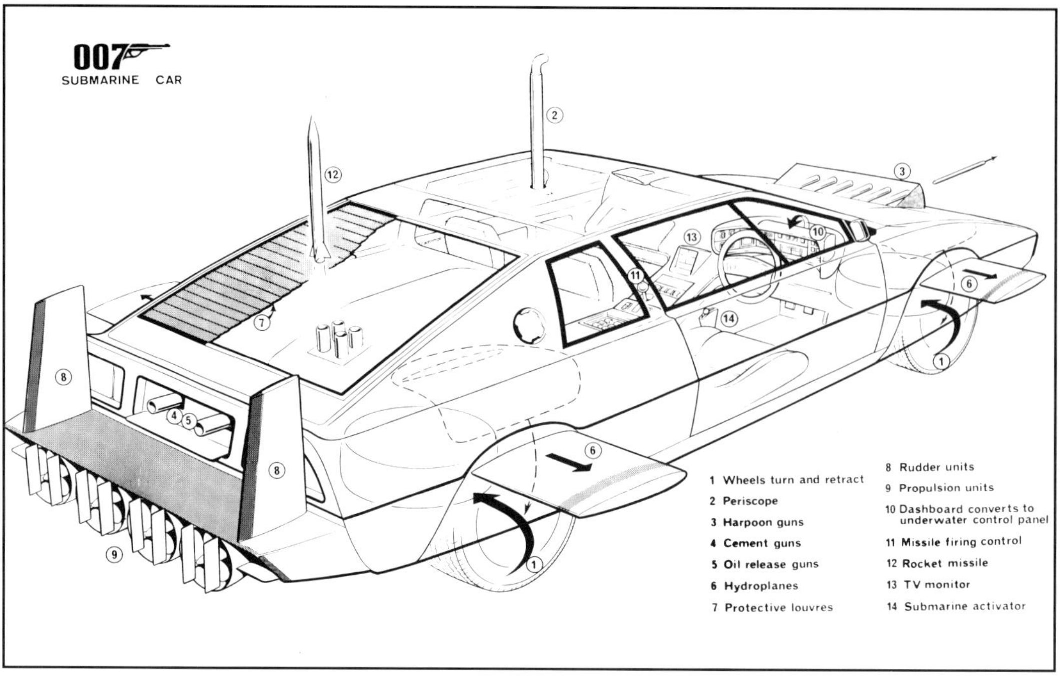

Plan of the Lotus submarine car from *The Spy Who Loved Me*.

- Linear induction tray.
- Impaling seat - knife in camel saddle. Ejector in pouffe.
- Special viewing apparatus.
- Machine gun Hookah.

MOONRAKER - 1979.

Producer -	ALBERT R. BROCCOLI
Director -	LEWIS GILBERT
007 -	ROGER MOORE
M -	BERNARD LEE
Q -	DESMOND LLEWELYN
Miss Moneypenny -	LOIS MAXWELL
Frederick Gray -	GEOFFREY KEEN

GADGETRY

- Special viewing equipment rigged up in M's office by Q.
- Cigarette lighter/camera.
- Hydrofoil.
- Wrist dart gun.
- Cigarette case X-ray apparatus for opening safe.
- Special Seiko watch with demolition apparatus and detonator.
- Special high speed Gondola and Hovercraft - called 'Bondola'.

- Q in Rio with laser gun (metal head).
- Siesta machine gun, giving the appearance of a man asleep wearing a sombrero.
- Powered hang glider.
- Q Boat with mine laying capabilities and homing torpedo.
- Exploding Bolas.

FOR YOUR EYES ONLY - 1981.

Producer -	ALBERT R. BROCCOLI
Director -	JOHN GLEN
007 -	ROGER MOORE
Q -	DESMOND LLEWELYN
Miss Moneypenny -	LOIS MAXWELL
Frederick Gray -	GEOFFREY KEEN

Due to the death of Bernard Lee, there is no M in this film.

GADGETRY

- Lotus Esprit with vibration sensors, magnetic seal points and four 1 lb. packs of explosives.
- 3D visual identigraph.
- Talon umbrella.
- Spring loaded arm cast.
- Binocular camera.
- Q's climbing equipment.
- Seiko watch with message inside dial.

OCTOPUSSY - 1983.

Producer -	ALBERT R. BROCCOLI
Director -	JOHN GLEN
007 -	ROGER MOORE
M -	ROBERT BROWN
Q -	DESMOND LLEWELYN
Miss Moneypenny -	LOIS MAXWELL
Frederick Gray -	GEOFFREY KEEN

GADGETRY

- Acrostar mini jet.
- Horsebox with false rear of a horse.
- Speeded up 3-wheeler auto rickshaw.
- Indian rope trick (Q's workshop India).

- Spiked door, opening with fatal force.
- TV watch and video camera.
- Homing device and microphone in Faberge egg.
- Homing device in watch.
- Mont Blanc fountain pen containing acid and receiver for bug in egg.
- Crocodile submarine for Bond.
- Q's hot air balloon with closed circuit TV cameras and receiver screen in basket.

A VIEW TO A KILL - 1985.

Producers -	ALBERT R. BROCCOLI AND MICHAEL G. WILSON
Director -	JOHN GLEN
007 -	ROGER MOORE
M -	ROBERT BROWN
Q -	DESMOND LLEWELYN
Miss Moneypenny -	LOIS MAXWELL
Frederick Gray -	GEOFFREY KEEN

GADGETRY

- Snooper - a small robot surveillance machine.
- Watch with garrotte cord.
- Fountain pen which causes the writing to burn.
- Polarising sunglasses.
- Ring with camera in centre.
- Bug detecting device under the head of an electric razor.
- A recorder.
- A video camera that transposes a cinema image into graphics and plots, from a central computer, the identity of the subject.

THE LIVING DAYLIGHTS - 1987.

Producers -	ALBERT R. BROCCOLI AND MICHAEL G. WILSON
Director -	JOHN GLEN
007 -	TIMOTHY DALTON
M -	ROBERT BROWN
Q -	DESMOND LLEWELYN
Miss Moneypenny -	CAROLINE BLISS
Frederick Gray -	GEOFFREY KEEN

GADGETRY

- The Aston Martin Volante with head-up visual display, scanning digital radio, special bullet-proof glass, fire-proof body, guided missiles, jet engine

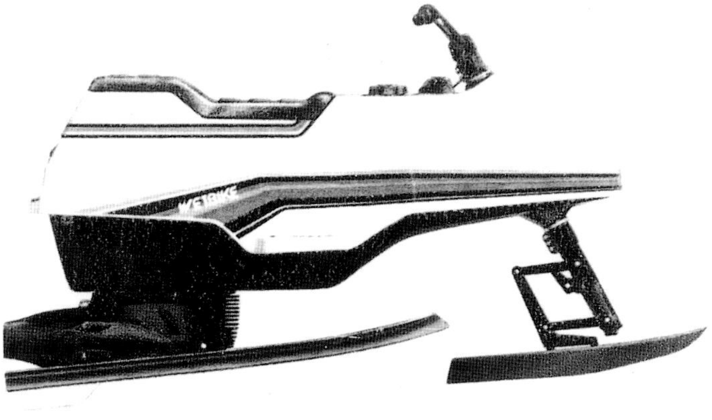

Wetbike Specifications

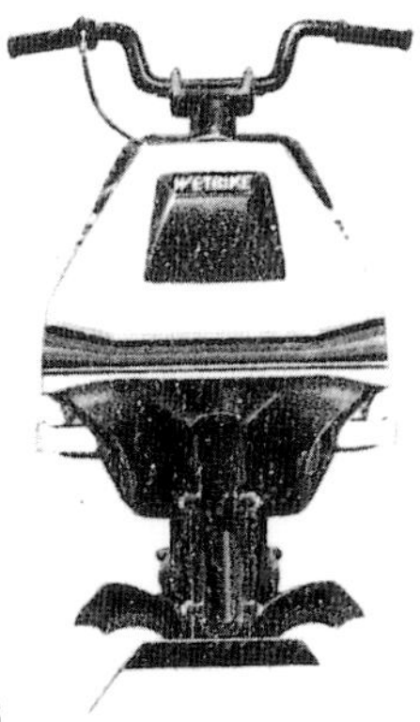

Length	
Hull	6 feet
Front to Rear Ski	7.5 feet
Width	2 feet
Height	
Hull	2.5 feet
Hull and Skis	3.5 feet
Draft	
Stationary	2 feet
Planing	3 inches
Weight	300 pounds
Gas Capacity	6 gallons
MPG	approximately 30
Maximum Speed	40 mph
0-40 mph	approximately 200 feet
Fuel Type	Oil and gas mixture (ratio 50:1)
Flotation Capacity	600 pounds
Engine Type	65 hp., 816cc
Body Fabrication	Fiberglass (¼-inch)
Seat Construction	Ensolite
Steering & Throttle	Aluminum
Skis	Aluminum (Front) Fiberglass (Rear)
Electrical System	12V, 60 AMP motorcycle battery

Specification of the Wet Bike. *The Spy Who Loved Me.*

booster rocket, weapons control panel, convertible ice tyres, special snow skis hidden in door sills, laser cutting device in wheel hubs, self-destruct mechanism.

- Rake metal detector.
- Sniper gear.
- Ghetto blaster - portable radio which fires mini rocket.
- Pen that duplicates what another pen writes by means of radio receiver.
- Couch which swallows its victims.
- Key ring which emits a stun gas together with a magnetic key ring finder, packed with highly concentrated explosives. Both are activated by whistling.

LICENCE TO KILL - 1989.

Producers -	ALBERT R. BROCCOLI AND MICHAEL G. WILSON
Director -	JOHN GLEN
007 -	TIMOTHY DALTON
M -	ROBERT BROWN
Q -	DESMOND LLEWELYN
Miss Moneypenny -	CAROLINE BLISS

GADGETRY

- Travel alarm clock packed with explosives.
- Standard British passport which detonates on opening.
- Hasselblad camera which can be broken apart and reconstructed as a signature gun.
- Cummerbund rappelling rope.
- Manta ray cover.
- Broom transmitter.
- Explosives disguised as toothpaste.
- Polaroid camera which shoots out laser beams and takes X-ray pictures.

GOLDENEYE - 1995.

Presented by -	ALBERT R. BROCCOLI
Producers -	MICHAEL G. WILSON AND BARBARA BROCCOLI
Director -	MARTIN CAMPBELL
007 -	PIERCE BROSNAN
M -	JUDI DENCH
Q -	DESMOND LLEWELYN
Miss Moneypenny -	SAMANTHA BOND

GADGETRY

- **Q** Leather belt with a piton and 75 foot rappelling cord built into buckle.
- **Q** Silver tray which doubles as a document scanner.
- **Q** Pen that becomes a class 4 grenade.
- **Q** Omega watch with laser that also serves as an arming device.
- **Q** Leg cast which becomes a missile launcher.
- **Q** Phone booth air bag.
- **Q** A digital camera - high resolution satellite transmitting camera.
- **Q** Key code override device.
- **Q** BMW (Z3) Roadster containing Stinger missiles, ejector seat, all-points radar and emergency parachute breaking.

TOMORROW NEVER DIES - 1997.

Producers -	MICHAEL G. WILSON AND BARBARA BROCCOLI
Director -	ROGER SPOTTISWOODE
007 -	PIERCE BROSNAN
M -	JUDI DENCH
Q -	DESMOND LLEWELYN
Miss Moneypenny -	SAMANTHA BOND

GADGETRY

- **Q** Another new car for Bond and this time it's a BMW 750 with a voice assisted navigation system, GPS tracking, a bullet-proof body, self inflating tyres, jets emitting tear gas, rack of rockets concealed in the sunroof, metal spikes behind rear bumper, metal cutter hidden under BMW badge. The bodywork produces 20,000 volt shocks to unauthorised personnel trying to force entry.
- **Q** Ericsson cellular phone with a device for scanning fingerprints, a laser beam, a lock pick, an activator for the 20,000 volt security system and the remote control pad.
- **Q** Dunhill cigarette lighter that becomes a grenade at the flick of a switch.
- **Q** An up-dated model of Bond's famous Walter PPK pistol - the P99.
- **Q** A detonator concealed in Omega watch with ignition system in rotary face.

THE WORLD IS NOT ENOUGH - 1999.

Producers -	MICHAEL G. WILSON AND BARBARA BROCCOLI
Director -	MICHAEL APTED
007 -	PIERCE BROSNAN
M -	JUDI DENCH
Q -	DESMOND LLEWELYN
R -	JOHN CLEESE
Miss Moneypenny -	SAMANTHA BOND

GADGETRY

- Q Reading glasses which create a blinding flash. Second pair with X-ray vision for checking concealed weapons.
- Q Hydro boat that operates in 3 inches of water.
- Q Bagpipes that fire bullets and double as a flamethrower.
- Q Watch holding dual lasers and miniature grappling hook with 50 feet of high-tensile micro-filament wire able to support 800 pounds.
- Q Air bag concealed in ski jacket.
- Q BMW (Z8) - the latest in intercepts, surveillance and countermeasures. Titanium plating and armour, missiles in headlamps and a multi-tasking head-up display. This includes a thin beam to pick up conversation at a distance and an infra-red tracking system. The vehicle is equipped with remote control.

BIBLIOGRAPHY

The Incredible World of 007. Lee Pfeiffer and Philip Lisa. 1992.

The Complete James Bond Movie Encyclopaedia. Steven Jay Rubin. 1990.

The Essential Bond. Lee Pfeiffer and Dave Worrall. 1998.

As You Were. Frank Slater. 1946.

South to Freedom. The Hon. T C F Prittie and Captain W Earle Edwards. 1946.

The Story of The 1st Battalion of The Royal Welch Fusiliers - May 10th to 27th, 1940. - First published in Y Ddraig Goch (the Regimental Journal) 1954 - 56.

The Man Who Was Q - The Life of Charles Fraser-Smith. David Porter. 1989.

No Ordinary Place. Christopher Hibbert. 1997.

Offlag. Don Quarrie. 1995.

Ian Fleming. Andrew Lycett. 1995.

When The Snow Melts. The Autobiography of Cubby Broccoli. Donald Zec. 1998.

South Wales Coal Mines 1840-1887.

AUTHOR'S NOTE

Historical researcher and antiques expert, Sandy Hernu, started writing about fifteen years ago. Since then she has had seven reference books published and is a regular contributor to various magazines on the subject of antiques. Friendship with Desmond kindled her long-time fascination for the James Bond 007 movies and resulted in this biography of the man behind Q.

INDEX